About the authors.

Richard Searle and Stephen Ritchie spent five weeks
at Number One in the British pop charts with the
record *Spirit in the Sky*, in the comedy psych-punk
garage-glam band Doctor and the Medics, touring
heavily throughout the nineteen eighties and surviving
much rock mischief.

Ritchie has since played in various bands,
including punk originals The Boys, TV Smith and
German stadium rockers Die Toten Hosen, and runs
his own record label called Drumming Monkey
Records.

Searle has also played with other bands,
including Acid Jazz funksters Corduroy, and has since
published a number of books.

Also by Richard Searle.

The Absurdist

Sketchistentialism

Richard Searle and Stephen Ritchie

The Memoirs of Damage & Vom
(Misadventures in Doctor and the Medics)

Forward

By Stephen Ritchie

The first time that I met Dickie Damage, was on New Year's Day in 1983. My old school friend, Julie Dartnell, told me about a show at the Queens Ballroom in Westcliff-on-Sea. The headliners were a band called Doctor and the Medics. I was out on a limb with nothing to do, so headed down to the station to accompany Julie to Southend. On arrival, I realised that I'd just missed Julie and the train by seconds, another half an hour in the freezing cold was the prospect awaiting me. With this in mind, I debated whether to suffer the elements, or go home and have an early night. That, there and then, was probably the biggest life changing decision that I ever made. I went to the gig.

On arrival at the Queens I managed to get in, meet Julie at the bar and order a beer, with just seconds to spare before The Medics hit the stage. That performance will stay with me forever. I was blown away. They started with a medley through the years called *The History Of Trash*, and it finished with The Cramps' *Human Fly*. The Cramps just happened to be my favourite band of the moment, and I had been listening to *Human Fly* minutes before I set off on my journey; a sign surely.

Despite some nerves, I headed back stage to talk to the band. Security was scarce, so I strolled into the dressing room and headed straight for the singer and said something stupid like...

'Are you into The Cramps?'

I was met with a vague and cryptic answer, which left me none the wiser. However, I discovered that there was another show scheduled a fortnight later in London, and, to top that, this hadn't been the normal drummer, they were in fact looking for a permanent replacement. This aroused my interest, and I said that I would be up for the job. The bass player overheard this and was not looking too happy. You have to consider that on this night I had green hair and was wearing a kilt, and this bass player in question was looking decidedly mod, albeit, with a bit of psychedelic beatnik thrown in. I moved on to him and was met with some semi-snide remarks.

My last train beckoned, so I bade them farewell, but whilst the door was still not fully closed, I heard some chuckling and unflattering comments, which were definitely coming from the bass player's corner. Somewhat deflated but still very keen for the job, it occurred to me that the bassist and I were probably not gonna be best buddies – I was to be proved wrong.

The years I spent with Doctor and the Medics were, without a doubt, some of the best and funniest times I've had in my life. I think the roller-coaster eventually came to a grinding halt for me after seven years, when I jumped ship and left the UK for greener pastures in New York (which I found not much greener, but that's another story). During that time there were fights, falling-outs, laughter and tears, but it all seemed wonderful at the time, and I loved every minute. It's strange as, even after all these years, I still have a

Medics dream at least once a week. I find myself in all sorts of situations with my old friends and wake up feeling slightly empty and sad that those days are over. Clive, Wendi, Steve, Colette, (also the Sues and Jane) and Richard (the semi-snide bassist mentioned above), were my family and friends for all those turbulent years, and I loved them (and still do). I'm amazed they put up with my lunacy for so long. I thank them dearly for that, and, on reflection, it's a miracle that we are all still around and doing well.

Richard (Dickie Damage - a nickname given for reasons which will become apparent on reading this book) mentioned the idea of writing a Medics memoir a few years ago. To begin with I wasn't overly enthusiastic, but I realised that it would be a marvellous excuse to get Mr D down the bar, laugh a lot and drink copious amounts of alcohol, whilst we discussed dates, times and details. Despite circumstances suggesting a somewhat difficult undertaking (my memory is such that my friends in Düsseldorf made me a t-shirt displaying my home address for taxi drivers), I was pleasantly surprised that my long-term memory remains relatively intact.

So, lovely people, strap yourselves in and prepare for a very unusual and eventful journey back in time. I wouldn't have missed it for the world.

Love, peace and bananas!

Vom

By the way:

We did not insult the Los Angeles Police Dept...we were in Miami.

The death threat was at the LA Roxy....not the Whiskey.

And...I did not steal that coffin lid!

V.

Richard Searle

The Memoirs Of Damage & Vom

'People with good memories seldom remember
anything worth remembering.'
anything worth remembering.'
(Anonymous)

1. Introduction

It was the first time that I had ever punched Mr Vom - and the last. The combined stress, alcohol and insanity of the day had taken their toll, something had to give. Vom didn't care, he had superpowers beyond the comprehension of mere mortals such as I; he groaned, picked some grasshopper legs from between his teeth and galloped back up the dirt track towards the scene of the crime. I squinted from a sudden glare of mountain sunlight and chased after him.

Fortunately, the Italian police had left, the routine formalities of arresting our flustered host completed (his court hearing was to be a few days later). The ambulance had gone also, taking the angry man whose leg our host had broken whilst fighting to protect the good name of his younger sister - who had just had sex in the woods with Mr Vom.

I noticed McGuire, still trying to get onto the small bandstand, miming *Spirit In The Sky* at the incensed accordion player, snatching the fragile squeeze-box with fingers shiny with sausage grease.

Colette was still in a semi-tearful state. I'd mistakenly told her of our host's confidential confession; he had romantic designs and had not envisaged having to house, feed and entertain three strange Englishmen when he agreed to her visit.

The yodelling man (the fiancé of our host's recently de-flowered sister) had seemed, just an hour or so earlier, genuinely entertained by the playful antics of Mr Vom (sticking cigarettes in his ears and nose, pogoing to the Bavarian oompah band and eating insects). But he, too, had now disappeared; a proud man who didn't speak English, who yodelled energetically to communicate with McGuire, Colette and myself, whilst his betrothed was having intercourse with Mr Vom.

As beer festivals went, this one was up there with the best, countless steins of delicious pilsner lager, plump bratwurst, traditional folk music and a good-natured family atmosphere in the scenic Italian Alps. But these simple, hard-working village people were no match for the demonic force of chaos that was Mr Vom, a Tasmanian-devil blur of banana-yellow pyjamas, spiky Ronald McDonald hair and punk rock cockery. We were only passing through, and it was time to leave; we were in danger of overstaying our welcome. We regrouped, said our goodbyes and hastened a victorious retreat.

'Good work, Mr Vom,' I said as we left.

'Sorry I chucked your sunglasses down the mountain, Dickie Damage,' he replied.

2. First impressions

I first met Mr Vom at Southend in Essex; he walked into our dressing room after a gig, except his name wasn't Vom - it was Stephen Ritchie. Announced before entering as 'keen to join the band', he was a drummer - we needed a drummer. In marched an undersized punk rocker with an oversized spiky haircut, a studded motorbike jacket and brothel creepers. He was friendly and smiley, with a positive attitude, but I sensed an aura of unbridled mischief about him; like an unexploded firework, lit but yet to take spark. He explained that he enjoyed bands like The Cramps; he thought that we were similar and promised to go to our next gig. I assumed that he was drunk or mad, and definitely dangerous.

A band is only as good as its drummer, and we'd been bad since we'd started. Initially formed at the tail-end of the post-mod revival, the 'new psychedelic' scene of 1981, based around a couple of clothes shops in Kensington Market (Sweet Charity and The Regal), plus a regular club night at the Soho dive Gossips (a small smoky basement in Meard Street, frequented by musicians, drunks and prostitutes) called The Clinic. The scene was cliquey and London-specific; it featured on the teatime television current affairs programme "Nationwide" as 'an emerging new youth cult'. The scene fizzled out shortly after.

The Clinic's resident DJ, Clive Jackson of Eltham (my Patrol Leader in the scouts), called himself The Doctor; freckled, be-spectacled, lank-haired and lanky, he was a great front man, funny as fuck and could almost hold a tune - almost. Clive was given an opportunity to make a record under the sole condition that the band name must be Doctor and the Medics. On guitar was Steve McGuire, a fleshy, bleach-haired, compost heap of a man. They recruited a hairdresser, Andy McLachlan, as a temporary drummer, not because he could drum but for free haircuts. With my good self on bass, a painfully shy teenager with bad skin and bouffant hair (I'd recently quit my previous band and lived locally), we were as much a band of social misfits as a group of musicians. After a handful of rehearsals, we recorded the barely playable single *The Druids Are Here / The Goats Are Trying To Kill Me* for Dan Treacy's Whaam! record label in 1982.

There was a 'New Psychedelic' compilation album released (through Warner) during the scene's demise, called *A Splash Of Colour* and featuring a scattering of the 'Clinic' bands, Miles Over Matter, Mood Six and The Marble Staircase plus others, some of which managed to sign major but short-lived record deals. The Medics were formed too late to make the running order but The Doctor made the cut, his trademark fake San Francisco dead-head alter-ego preaching to the converted through an ocean of slap-back echo.

The Medics' hairdresser was replaced after a handful of gigs, some spectacularly bad, but fun enough for Phil Ward, the lead singer of (recently dropped from EMI Records) Mood Six, to take an interest. He too

14

could drum a little, and we continued our shambolic mission.

From the beginning, the awkwardly limbed Jackson acquired girlfriends by inviting them to sing backing vocals for 'his' band. The pear-shaped Lewisham lovely Fiona Crompton was first, but somewhere down the line the Southend contingent became involved. Wendi West made clothes for Sweet Charity and dated Gary Simpson (the singer of Essex band Le Mat), both of whom had shared a converted Kentish oast house with Jackson. Wendi became unattached, and Clive asked her to sing. Some years our elder, Wendi was a woman without hips, chest or other lady curves; stick thin and foul-mouthed with long black frizzy hair and a button nose. Wendi introduced us to Jane (the petite ex-girlfriend of Pete Helmer, the guitarist from Le Mat) and another oast house resident and ex-con, 'Old Sue'. They donned long black wigs, psychedelic make-up and called themselves The Anadin Brothers (so called because of their constant headaches and an uncanny resemblance to men in drag). The singing was on occasion appalling, the smell of patchouli oil often overpowering, but they helped to divert attention from The Doctor's voice.

Phil Ward couldn't make a gig on one occasion, in Southend. The drummer from Le Mat, Sav, was asked to fill in; he really could drum. This was the gig that local punk Stephen Ritchie attended, and Sav was partly the reason why it had impressed him (we weren't usually that good). Ritchie played with a couple of bands; Clive went to see one and phoned me up immediately after.

'Really, he's brilliant,' he promised, 'like Keith Moon.'

Phil Ward returned for our next gig, at the Ad Lib club in Kensington. Stephen Ritchie came to watch. He was sporting his office suit, still with his trademark hair and creepers. We chatted at the bar, I insisted that he must attend the next five gigs in a row, by way of initiation, which he agreed to do. There was one problem: his name. McGuire was also Steve, and people sometimes called me Richie (short for Richard); he needed a nickname. A recent TV show called "Bad News", by The Comedy Strip (a Spinal Tap style band spoof) featured a character called Vim. I changed one letter, and that's how Vom got the name; it suited him well. It sounded short for vomit... perfect.

Ward realised his days were numbered and bowed out gracefully. Mr Vom was in and was incredible; and I would, from that moment onwards, be spat at in rehearsals, have my beer spiked, my flat trashed, my liver punished and my life put at risk. My sanity and dignity would be put to the test, but I was a musician, a Medic and a mod and about to set forth on an adventure in which Mr Vom would be pivotal.

3. Drunk Rock

Just how drunk do you have to get before it is considered unacceptable? Well, ...that seems to depend very much upon timing. I have seen a barely conscious and very naked Mr Vom rugby tackle the backing-singers, mid-song, during a King's College ball in London's Strand, and no-one think anything of it. Yet similar antics would receive torrents of verbal abuse and physical threats at earlier shows.

Bad behaviour did not go down well when the band was struggling for recognition. This was, however, not always the case. At a very early gig (pre-Vom) with the hairdresser behind the drums, at a club/pub called The Mitre (south side of the Blackwall Tunnel), everything went wrong. The venue was flooded (blocked drains) and smelt, the stage collapsed, the band were drunk on budget lager. We couldn't finish a single song without something messing up. The crowd loved it. We were supported by cockney gob-jockey, Billy Bragg, who stood open-mouthed in bemusement as he witnessed disarray and un-professionalism applauded. Flushed with success, fresh faced and sweating from our stage exertions, we considered it a triumph. That was good timing.

Once we realised that our 'trashy' sound could draw a crowd, we worked this chaotic performance into the act. The girls' odd and scary choreography became stranger and curiously focused. The songs were tailored to suit a 'rocky horror show'

17

brief; played with passion by McGuire and myself. Clive crafted his caterwauling, creating a stage persona based on Jim Morrison and Elvis Presley. His theatrical clothing became more exaggerated and extreme (one pair of custom-made velvet trousers featured a cut-away gusset to display his pubic hair that he'd dyed bright pink). Mr Vom, when peering from behind his over-sized drum kit, provided the final flourish to the pandemonium; with arms flailing and cymbals splashing, the gyroscopic head-banging nut-case perfected the ensemble, but he did like a drink.

A brooding gentleman named James Bloomer, the entertainment secretary at Hampstead College and a Territorial Army enthusiast, offered to manage us. He had a sombre nature, which was put to good effect when threatening Vom into staying 'sober' before stage time. With James' input we worked hard to be noticed, to get our break; recording basic demos, constructing the set properly; he was taking us to the 'right' parties and arranging gigs. He gave us focus; all we needed was a review in the music press.

James had to eventually step aside (to concentrate on his guns), but as a parting gift he arranged for a journalist from *Time Out* magazine to review a forthcoming show at The Rock Garden in London's Covent Garden. We were confident that our carefully honed act would electrify the journo, but just to be safe James had arranged for a warm-up gig a few days before, at Chelsea Art College, to make sure we were properly prepared.

To kill time between the band sound-check and stage time, Mr Vom and I sat in a prime location in the student bar, watching trendy artist girls and enjoying the subsidised watered-down bitter. We were particularly enjoying the beer, a light and flavoursome ale that went down a treat and raised our spirits.

Come stage time we'd each consumed eight pints of the delicious beer and felt boss. The performance was one of our best to date. Mr Vom's drumming was fluid and loose, and my often shy and self-conscious stage presence felt more relaxed. In fact, I really got into it, swinging my bass around, playfully backing into Clive and grooving along with the Anadin Brothers' routines. Mr Vom later commented that I was 'at my best' and should always drink eight pints before a concert; I made a mental note of this advice.

Come the day of the all-important Rock Garden gig we were all in fine fettle. A *Time Out* review was the missing link to our ultimate success; we were sure that we'd impress. James threatened Mr Vom (one last time) to remain sober until after the gig. The promoter was very pleased, the show was sold out, the sound-check was fine, and some friends turned up for moral support. An old chum, Mathew Lily (a kid who lived down my street), appeared after sound-check, and we went to a local pub to chat and catch up on old gossip.

The Nags Head in James Street was a lively pub that had a good atmosphere and didn't water down its beer. I took a liking to a continental lager, served from an ornate pump; it was delicious, full-bodied and strong. Various band members floated in and out to meet friends as I sat and talked with my pal Mathew. Clive noticed the collection of empty beer glasses building up on our table.

'Don't get drunk,' he warned, 'it's an important gig.'
I'd only had three pints.

'Don't worry,' I assured him, 'three pints and I'm good.'

The hours passed, and the fresh lager was invigorating. Clive reappeared and commented on my appearance.

'You look pissed,' he barked.

I'd only had five pints.

'Don't worry,' I reasoned, 'three pints, I'm good, five pints and I'm great.'

Stage time approached, and I was fully enjoying the pub ambiance. Clive marched back in.

'Stop drinking,' he ordered.

I'd met my perfect eight pint quota.

'Don't worry, three pints, I'm good, five pints and I'm great, but eight pints and I'm at my very best.' I slurred.

We were to be introduced on stage by a beat-poet. As a jazz fan, I was asked to accompany him with some walking bass lines whilst he bop-talked in rhyming Kerouac style. The packed Rock Garden audience clapped with delight as I crouched behind the poet, the volume control on my bass guitar turned half-way down, so as not to drown out the poetry. It seemed to be going well.

'Scabaah-scroony, a-scab-bab-aroony - like crazy Daddio,' chanted the beatnik.

My little friend, Mathew Lily, shouted up from the audience.

'Turn it up, Rich,' he cried, 'we can't hear you.'

I moved over to my amp and cranked up the volume knob a few notches as the crowd roared the full band on-stage. Clive held his arms aloft in recognition of people's enthusiasm. Mr Vom counted in, and we burst into the opening number. I noticed that the volume control on my bass was turned half way down, that wasn't right. In the nick of time, I turned it up full and thudded away, swinging my bass around, playfully backing into Clive and grooving along with The Anadin Brothers' routines – fully confident that I was 'at my best'.

Oblivious to the size of the tiny stage and the booming volume of my instrument, I collided, bashed, stumbled and thoroughly annoyed the band. I was, it transpired, quite drunk. The girls began pummelling my kidneys from the rear and twisting my tuning keys from the front, infuriated by my behaviour. No one could hear themselves on stage, including me. I was far too loud (and out of tune). Mr Vom climbed from his kit mid-way through the song and switched off my amp.

'Listen to what you're playing,' he shouted. I kicked my amplifier, confused as to why it had cut out; I flicked all the knobs and cranked it up even further as it miraculously sparked back into life. As the first song stopped the audience stood silently, open-mouthed in bemusement as they witnessed disarray and un-professionalism that could never be applauded; Mr Vom kicked over his drums and stormed off stage, Clive and the girls following closely behind.

I packed away my equipment and went backstage, just in time to see Clive punch McGuire in the face, the result of an ill-timed comment from McGuire, who'd also had a few too many beers. James had already disappeared, disgusted by this wasted opportunity; we'd never see him again. The girls were throwing up in the toilet, also the worse for wear. Mr Vom packed his things and left, furious. He'd remained completely sober for the gig; the only one who had done so.

The audience got their money back, and the promoter charged the band for a broken microphone stand (destroyed whilst I stomped about the stage, it was presented to me as a trophy of shame). We did not receive our review in *Time Out*. That was bad timing.

Many years later, when a totally drunk, nude and rude Mr Vom threw his drum sticks in the air halfway through a song, the better to leap from his drum stool and wrestle an Anadin Brother to the ground, darting back and forth across the stage, skidding and sliding in spilt beer and sweat, bollock-naked and as pissed as a wankered Russian, no-one minded nor cared, especially Mr Vom, who thoroughly enjoyed himself. The audience didn't bat an eye; they had other things to see and do, and, crucially, they were pissed as well.

That is the answer, the key; if nobody objects, if no-one cares that you are drunk, only then can you get away with it. That is good timing.

4. Out Of It

'All hail *the out of it cup*, ahhh, ahhhh, ahh,' whimpered the barely audible Mr Vom before his legs crumpled, and he collapsed into an unconscious, dribbling tangle of boneless limbs and hair-lacquered fuzz. The rest of the room sighed relief and concentrated on the few remaining hours of precious sleep.

Once absorbed into The Medics, Vom quickly established himself as a manic, chaotic but solid drummer, though one whose reputation was that of, when given half a chance, a nuisance. However, gigs were getting better, as was the quality of venues;

audiences were happy, and things quickly progressed. A proper band at last, people began to take notice.

Clive was befriended around this period by a mousey-haired, beak-nosed chap by the curious name of Roman Jugg; he played keyboards and then, soon after, guitar for punk rock originators The Damned. Roman hung out with The Medics, produced some demos and performed with us on stage a few times. Almost famous, he became our guru.

Thanks to Roman, we were invited to support The Damned at an outdoor festival at Nostell Priory in Leeds. In addition, McGuire could play keyboards on The Damned's encore; as such (as a member of The Damned) he'd get a hotel room.

We arrived in Leeds late at night; we planned to sneak in and sleep on McGuire's floor. We shook security without problem. The room was tiny, but everyone found floor space and settled down for the night. However, Vom discovered a small Formica fronted fridge. We huddled around, intrigued by its multi-coloured contents. It was called a 'mini-bar', the first we'd ever seen. It contained:

2 x 50cl bottle of white wine
2 x 50cl bottle of red wine
2 x 50cl bottle of Gordon's Gin
2 x 35cl bottle of Bacardi Rum
2 x 35cl bottle of Courvoisier Cognac
2 x 35cl bottle of Famous Grouse Whisky
2 x 50cl bottle of Smirnoff Vodka
1 x 20cl bottle of Grand Marnier
2 x small can of Carlsberg Lager
2 x small can of Coke
2 x 50cl bottle of Schweppes Tonic Water
2 x bottle of mineral water

4 Ritz Crackers and a tin of nuts

In no particular order, ignoring McGuire's concerns about prices and fearless to the perils of mixing spirits, Mr Vom methodically worked his way through the contents. He utilised a minty toothbrush mug from the bathroom, then sipped and savoured every last drop of the (apparently gratis) wealth of alcohol - quaffed from the mighty chalice that he named *'the out of it cup'*.

McGuire lumped out of bed, over the sprawling bodies, and briefly studied a vinyl clad menu from the fridge door.

'It isn't free,' he moaned, 'you're paying for it.'

Vom ignored this mirth shattering news, too drunk to care; he chimed out a final hymn to the gods of drink.

'All hail the out of it cup...ahhhhh,' and swallowed the final drops; his body buckling from fatigue and toxin. We could finally rest.

Next morning, news of Mr Vom's mini-bar achievement circulated quickly. It turned out that mini-bars are very expensive, 'it was very serious'. Roman told McGuire that the bill would be deducted from our band fee, which was less than the mini-bar bill.

The gig was great, and we celebrated hard. The beer sped straight to our heads, we'd hardly eaten, so decided to explore the stalls at the back of the muddy field in search of burgers. Hidden amongst the potent fug of smouldering joss sticks, within a market-trader maze of cheese-cloth shirts and dream catchers, appeared a solitary table with rectangular slabs of brown candied sugar and a hand written sign, 'Hash Toffee £2'. I had enough money for a burger or a piece of toffee. Mr Vom advised that I invest in dessert. We paid our money and unpeeled the cling-film wrapping. The block of sweet, sticky toffee smelt pungent and outdoorsy. With the rich velvety texture of treacle, yet crumbly and crystalline like home-made Devon fudge, it tasted wonderful and provided my rumbling stomach with just enough lining to continue drinking.

As we were bussed back to the hotel, we finalised plans to once more avoid staff and crash in McGuire's room, but we'd party for a while in the hotel bar with The Damned. We were instructed to keep a low profile.

The bar buzzed with gentle laughter and well-behaved banter; I sat on an unusually vivid purple sofa by myself and practised keeping a low profile. I could still taste the crunchy brown sugar as I sucked caramel from between my teeth, my tongue polishing the enamel to savour every last morsel - a never ending task as it turned out. My molars seemed to be massive, far too big for my mouth. I considered measuring them against my fingers, but they too were huge, strange rippling lengths of bony flesh attached to big paddle hands. I peered anxiously about the gaudy neon-lit bar, why was everyone looking at me? Confused and panic-stricken, electricity crackled audibly around my brain. I did not feel right. Then, in what seemed like one orchestrated murmur, I heard an ancient chant on the hotel bar breeze.

'Hassshhhhh Toffffeeeee.'
The spirits of the sweets gently reassured me - hash toffee contains hashish. The drug was strong, and I was hallucinating but would be ok. My body slumped, and I relaxed into the experience.

Out of the corner of my eye I noticed McGuire surreptitiously mooching off to his room, he'd had the toffee too. Wendi was laughing hysterically at a foil ash tray, and Clive looked like he was ironing his face with his hand. Dave Vanian (The Damned's vampire obsessed singer) looked freakish and fascinating; chalk-skinned, black-eyed and raven-haired, with silver flames flicking around his elfin ears.

I noticed Rat Scabies (The Damned drummer) circling Vom, scratching the carpet with his feet. Suddenly his arm shot out like he was snatching a piece of stale cheese. Slap! The sharp sound cut the mood. Scabies slapped Vom hard around the cheek.

'That's for thieving from mini-bars,' he hissed.
Vom raised himself to his full tip-toed height.

'You can't hit me, I'm only five foot three,' he complained.
Slap! Scabies did it again, hunching over Mr Vom like a feeding rodent.

I realised that the bar had otherwise fallen completely silent, and that I was gliding towards the commotion. My limbs felt long and heavy. Scabies watched as I floated past him and sat down near Vom, who plopped down next to me; the bemused participant of his own toffee misadventure. Scabies sat opposite, silently searching my dilated pupils for signs of provocation.

'He's alright,' someone said, 'he's had the hash toffee.'
I turned away and continued my meditations; the better to observe Dave Vanian's hair (the reason for my seating rearrangement). Once Scabies realised that I was harmless, he scuttled away, sniffing the air for attention.

Fatigue suddenly began to weigh heavily upon me; it was Clive tapping my shoulder.

'McGuire's disappeared,' he said wearily, 'we'll have to sleep in the van.'

We slept as best we could in the freezing Avis Hire transit van. Mr Vom joined us, the promoter having paid the mini-bar bill; he was forgiven.

We were entertained on the return journey by Rat Scabies, already pissed. His eye-balls were blood-shot and swollen; the result of boasting that he could open a beer bottle in twenty different ways. He managed three - with a lighter, a bottle opener and, without success, his eye sockets. He stole the beer from the mini-bars of checked-out hotel guests.

5. Grotty

Clive lived in a large one room bedsit in an old Victorian house in Shooters Hill Road on Blackheath. It always smelt strange. He called it his 'fairly grotty fairy grotto', which didn't really explain the smell but was otherwise accurate. He shared the room with various people over the years, Marco, a local lothario, Martin Pyle, our roadie/tour manager and occasional controller of the Audio Generator (an antiquated synthesizer that produced a single throbbing pulse that made the audience nauseous), and, eventually, Wendi West from The Anadin Brothers, whom he would later marry. The flat-mates changed but nothing else did, the room was a palace of ink, music and scum.

The walls were covered in concert flyers and (mostly nude and disfigured) life drawings from the pen of Clive himself. His records were stored in plastic crates positioned nearby the constantly played seventies hi-fi; slotted between two mattresses, gas-fire and a basic kitchenette. Before the band could afford storage for equipment, drums, guitars and amps were sometimes stored in a wardrobe next to the sink, his clothes squashed between. A tatty tartan curtain was drawn across the front to neaten the mess.

If you had the pleasure of crashing on his floor overnight, which many people did, especially Mr Vom, you would be offered peanut butter on toast for breakfast, from a jar that was kept especially for guests. Clive would never partake from this jar; he and

Martin farted in it as soon as they awoke each morning without fail, unless, of course, they had guests. If you needed the lavatory, it was situated outside the room. The small hallway bathroom-toilet, shared with other flats, was Spartan except for a toilet-roll holder and a container of talcum powder... that Mr Vom liked to secretly urinate in.

Within this bedsit many of the early Medics songs were written by Clive, McGuire and myself; Mr Vom and the girls' contributions were added later in rehearsal. Weird alcohols and other more exotic medicines were occasionally consumed within these walls, LSD, Psilocybin mushrooms and Mescal. But most importantly Clive's place was our rendezvous point before gigs. When we could afford it, the band van (the Medics-mobile) was parked outside. On gig days Clive was often in bed when we arrived to load the van, never a nice sight, flies buzzed around his arse crack until he finally dressed. As such we were accustomed to his inappropriate nudity, unsanitary habits and bottom trickery.

Clive had several party tricks; the least offensive was the 'continuous raspberry'. He had mastered a constant breathing technique (apparently useful for playing a didgeridoo) that consisted of exhaling through his pursed lips (a raspberry) whilst inhaling through his nose in a circular motion. We learnt to stand aside when he did this, to avoid the spray of saliva.

Next in his routine was the 'testicular rotation'. He could twist his bollocks around five times; the resulting effect looked like an over-ripe aubergine about to pop. Mr Vom often tried to imitate this feat of ball-bag athleticism, but Clive had the advantage, his genitals were stretched and saggy through years of manhandling.

The last of the wacky Doctor's party performances, and by far the least pleasant, was 'knocking at the door', which once gave me nightmares. To successfully achieve 'knocking at the door' required a dinner plate, saucer or upturned biscuit tin lid, although an empty Kentucky Fried Chicken box was on one occasion successfully utilised, and that's it really. (It was advisable, if possible, to leave the room entirely when the activity was about to commence, or hide behind furniture if available. At the very least turn away, and shut your eyes.) The procedure worked as follows: Clive removed any unnecessary garments (trousers and underwear) from his person, then bent down, legs apart, as if to touch his toes. He positioned the dinner plate carefully between his inner thighs and pushed his bowels. Initially nothing happened, just some moist noises and possibly the odd splash of wet brown; then followed his narration, dramatic and deliberate.

'Behold.'

A small turd then squeezed from his anus, like a tortoise head peering cautiously from its shell, becoming larger as it emerged from within. The stink would at this point be horrendous.

'Ladies and gentlemen,' he would say proudly, 'I give you - knocking at the door.'

He'd wait for a ripple of recognition, only then, as the semi-executed stool waved precariously about his dirty buttocks, would he attempt to suck it back inside his hellish orifice before it escaped completely and plopped onto the plate; usually accompanied by screams of dread and horror.

This darkest of deeds, these ablutions of a terrible soul, this routine of a fiendish unwashed hippy, ensured that no-one, ever, overstayed their welcome in the fairly grotty fairy grotto.

6. Batcave

The Batcave was a proto-Goth nightclub started in 1982, also at Gossips, that had a style culture, which ran parallel to the 'new-psychedelic' scene based around The Clinic. 'Batcavers' shared some musical influences with the 'psychs' (Alice Cooper, The Damned and The Cramps) and as such, when The Batcave moved to Fouberts (in Fouberts Place, just off of Carnaby St), The Medics were invited to play.

Despite being a late-opening club, with an 11.30pm stage time, the sound-check was at 4pm in the afternoon; the club was very strict about this. Clive hired a transit van, we loaded the equipment, McGuire and myself squeezed into the back, and we set off from his flat at around 2pm, plenty of contingency time; Martin Pyle was at the wheel (Clive had a migraine so didn't want to drive). Mr Vom and the girls were to meet us there.

We made good time until we crossed Westminster Bridge, but then a police car waved us over for a routine check. One policeman asked us to stand on the pavement whilst he checked the driver's documents; the other inspected the contents of the van. Everything seemed fine until the copper noticed that Clive's name was on the van hire documents and Martin was driving.

'It's a fair cop,' Clive admitted, 'I have a bad migraine so Martin offered to drive.'

The copper seemed genuinely amused on hearing somebody actually say 'it's a fair cop' and was just about to let us go, when the other policeman pulled a tin from a tatty holdall that contained McGuire's guitar leads; a small white pill tin with a picture of the fictional children's character Winnie the Pooh on the lid. He carefully opened the tin, inside was a solitary slimming pill, Dexedrine; the yellow peril, a 'Dexie' - speed.

The police called for back-up, and we were read our rights. A wagon arrived minutes later with four other officers seated in the rear; we were positioned between them and sped towards Charing Cross Police Station. At the station we were asked who the pill belonged to? We all looked at McGuire to speak up; he didn't. They then questioned us individually, asking the same question.

'Whom does the pill belong to?'

'It isn't mine,' we each replied.

The booking sergeant gave us one last chance.

'Just admit who it belongs to, they'll get a caution, and you can all be on your way.'

Clive, Martin, every policeman in the room and I stared at McGuire - the owner of the holdall (with his name written on it) containing the slimming pill. We said nothing and so did McGuire.

We were each processed, strip-searched and put into individual cells. There was a drunken Scotsman already in mine, who lunged at me with his big tattooed fists, but he was over-powered by the police, and I was shown into another cell. We were not going to make our strict 4pm sound-check

Night fell, and the cells were needed for the 'after the pub' session. We were released, each with a caution; it was 11 o'clock. We sped to Fouberts, met the others, set up the gear, changed our shirts, plugged in our guitars and burst into our opening number as the clock struck 11.30; we'd just made it.

'Why the fuck didn't you just admit that the pill was yours?' Clive asked McGuire on the drive home.
    'I knew they couldn't prove it was mine; I wasn't bothered. I had a good sleep in my cell actually, I felt really refreshed for the gig.'

Arrested, strip-searched, cautioned, attacked by a drunk, six hours spent pacing back and forth in a damp grey concrete police cell that stank of bleach and piss; but McGuire had a nice nap - so that was alright then.

7. Stonehenge

The first thing I saw when we arrived at the
Stonehenge Festival was a naked man with a bright
white penis, a can of grease paint in one hand and a
blob of white stuff on the tip of his index finger.

'Protect your cock against sunburn, free,' he
offered. He waggled his finger at us as we passed.
'Cock paint?' We didn't need penis sun protection and
declined his generosity.

Having negotiated other equally curious
oddballs and avoided eye contact with several Hells
Angels, we parked the van in a lower field at the edge
of the main activity. We were booked to play on one of
the many stages that evening but had a few hours to
explore and absorb the insanity of humanity's outcasts
having a humongous free party. Clive and the girls
headed towards the hippy clothing stalls, overflowing
with Afghan coats and love beads. McGuire and I went
off in search of LSD. Mr Vom ran back to find the
penis paint man.

I had never taken Acid up until this point; I
was convinced that Stonehenge, with its flower-child
and quasi-Druidic traditions would be the perfect place
to start, McGuire also. Almost immediately we came
across a handwritten cardboard sign advertising
'dRuGs'. We both purchased a single transparent
gelatine square from a wizened biker, awkwardly cut
with tailoring scissors from a larger clear Acid-soaked
sheet. The wizard said they were 'windowpanes'. We
carefully placed the tiny translucent tabs in our

wallets, to consume after the gig, and headed back to base in time to catch Mr Vom showing off his freshly whitened penis.

Stonehenge was like no other event, with a complete absence of corporate sponsorship, logo branding, concert promoters or ticket stalls; it was the anything goes festival. A shanty-town of makeshift stages, stalls and theatre spaces arranged in haphazard rows and avenues. Music played everywhere, at all times and from every direction. Opportunist bands performed on backs of trucks, powered by car batteries and petrol-driven generators, creating a blend of rhythms and styles as you passed from one bank of speakers to the next. Speed metal merging with psychedelic rock fading into punk, it was chaos but utterly incredible. Clive noticed a sign propped in front of a pile of beer crates. 'The Invisible Band - tonight at midnight,' it said mysteriously. Convinced that this was a reformed psychedelic rock band from the late nineteen sixties, we set our minds to return at midnight.

A thin wire boundary fence marked the edge of the field where we camped. The next field down (empty when we arrived) had been put to full use as a public toilet. There were no portaloo cubical blocks at Stonehenge, people shat wherever they wanted. The convenience of the 'shitting field' meant that you could simply squat down behind a clump of grass to preserve your modesty and defecate to your heart's content. Obviously you had to be careful where you walked, but we too made full use of this land with our own ablutions. We each took a nervous shit before stage time, changed into our favourite hippy/biker-friendly outfits and steeled ourselves to perform before the pagan freaks of the Stonehenge solstice.

Stonehenge clapped and cheered in all the right places, and we left the stage and audience happy, if a little confused. We regrouped back at the campsite, consumed lager, dissolved windowpanes on our tongue, gathered supplies and ventured forth to watch The Invisible Band.

The festival came alive at night, lit only by the flames and lamps of its transitory residents; it throbbed and glowed with a warm orange pulse. Halogen bulbs buzzed blue-white light that blended into the flickering yellows and shadowy purples of camp-fires and petrol-daubed torches. The sound was intense. Motorbike engines revved in beat with the cacophony of music, laughter, crying, screaming, shouting, whispering, whimpering and more music. As we wandered through the mass of partially lit figures, I could feel my chest tightening, an odd pressure somewhere under my ribs, which Wendi explained was the Acid working. Faces in the crowd seemed to be watching me closely; eyeballs, large and watery, examined my every movement. I zipped up my American fish-tail parka to protect myself from the scrutiny of the strange folk, who weren't on my trip. A wave of paranoia invaded my thoughts in a sudden rush of clarity. 'You're dressed like a mod - surrounded by Hells Angles,' I heard myself thinking out loud. Wendi grabbed my sleeve and pulled me from my momentary panic, and I noticed a hot-dog wagon smiling at me. It was a VW camper van with hatches in the side that flapped like dragonfly wings, hovering up and down to the pulse of the music. Its headlights winked, and its radiator grill fixed a friendly grin in my direction, everything was okay.

We arrived at our destination. A stage of beer crates, the mysterious sign that announced the second coming of The Invisible Band, and a small crowd that had already gathered; it was midnight. Familiar ambient rock music boomed from the stage, a solitary naked figure, smeared in body paint, writhed and contorted to the sound of the song; the musicians hidden out of our sight, invisible.

'The Invisible Band,' Clive quietly mused in awe of this epic event, as we eventually returned to our camp-site. We gathered wood from other people's empty camp-sites and built a warming fire. We sat or slept through the night, Clive stoking the flames.

'I am Quark, keeper of the flame,' he repeated, speedily.
I rested against a fence post and watched as the last log burnt, and the sun began to rise.

As I came down from my trip and the sunlight reddened my face, we loaded the van and left, exhausted but satisfied. We realised that the reunion performance of The Invisible Band was actually just a naked man dancing along to a Hawkwind cassette playing from a boogie box. There was no band, invisible or otherwise. There was however hundreds of fresh-faced festival goers who were arriving that morning, and they were all setting up their tents in the shitting field.

8. Paris

Paris - city of love, cool jazz and car crashes. Our first
booking abroad, we were to play a gig in a popular
nightclub in one of the seedier districts of Paris; we
were very excited. Booked on a late crossing from
Dover, we had a warm-up gig in the Brighton Escape
club (a small beach-road venue) the evening before.
There was plenty of time to make the ferry, and we
enjoyed the gig, thrilled about our Parisian
rendezvous.

As the Brighton venue was shutting, we
managed to illicitly secure several beverages from
behind the bar. This was a delicate and dangerous
procedure at which we would become quite adept; the
operation would go like this. Someone would cause a
distraction; my preferred technique was to strip, which
usually worked well (except for one time in an Italian
lesbian bar). Once staff attention was diverted, two
band members (this was the optimum number for
speed and efficiency) would dart behind the bar and
pilfer as many drinks as possible. We would then exit
the venue, jump in the van and leave the scene of the
crime.

As we sped away from Brighton, we
examined our booty, some bottles of white wine, a few
beers and a bottle of cheap vodka. The reluctance to
touch the vodka and the inevitable squabble over the
beer led to the creation of one of the finest drinking
games that mankind will ever conceive, Swig and

Swap. The rules of this ingenious amusement are as follows:

The players sit in a circle; each receives a bottle from the available selection. A responsible adult is selected as Swig Master, who does not take a bottle. Each player holds the opened bottle in his or her right hand. The Swig Master gives the first command.

'Swig!'

The players drink from their respective bottle, until the Swig Master gives the second command.

'Swap!'

At which point the players thrust their bottle into the middle of the circle, whist at the same time snatching another bottle with the left hand. The commands are repeated.

'Swig! Swap!' until the bottles are empty. A lucky player will grab the drinks with the weaker alcohol content, beer or wine, the unlucky the vodka. There is no way of guaranteeing which bottle you end up with, especially as you get inevitably more and more intoxicated, which happens at an alarming speed. We played several rounds of Swig and Swap whilst the van hurried towards Dover.

A night-fog began to settle and the Medics-mobile became quickly lost amongst the B-roads and hedges of the south coast. We didn't care in the back, we were merry and oblivious. There was a slight whine of concern from the driver, Alex 'Binky' Bienkov (my Scout leader) and roadie Martin 'Piley' Pyle that we wouldn't make the ferry in time, which grew into a full-on major complaint when the van broke down on a secluded country lane miles away from anywhere.

The pause for the AA man to repair the vehicle gave its occupants an urgently needed toilet stop, which was when we noticed that it was foggy, and the van had broken.

The mechanic looked on in bewilderment, as a gibbering bunch of paralytic reprobates urinated over everything and anything; emptying bladders of the evening's fluids, unabashed, unashamed, falling-over-drunk, skirts-hitched, trousers-down and giggling. We missed the ferry, obviously.

Once checked into our hotel the next day, having slept off the booze as best we could, we refreshed ourselves for a night of Parisian hospitality. Driving around the heart of Paris, *Take Five* by Dave Brubeck on repeat in the music system, we were up for French fun.

Our host arranged to meet us in a fantastic bohemian bar called The Piano Vache (piano cow). It was brilliant. Waxed Courvoisier bottle candles flickered green light across torn sheet music pasted to the walls, red wine flowed with plentiful supplies of Leffe beer in large glass goblets; all accompanied by a constant soundtrack of quality Be-Bop. I loved it. It was beatnik heaven; beautiful pale-faced girls with ironed hair discussed Camus with goateed pseudo-existentialist boyfriends amongst the heavy aromatic cloak of Gauloises cigarettes and a faint whiff of garlic. We pretended to be intellectual and got profoundly drunk.

The next morning I was vaguely aware of chatter in the hotel room. My bed was nearest the door. Bienkov was standing in the doorway, hands animated, talking over my head to McGuire in the bed next to me. Also present was Mr Vom, who had crashed on our floor, too wrecked to reach his own room. Sleep and blood-alcohol levels prevented me from following the discussion; I sat up in bed, smacked my lips, announced that my mouth was dry, then fell back into a deep boozy doze.

'I hate you sometimes, Dickie,' Mr Vom spluttered as he followed Bienkov out of the room.

'Richard... Richard... Richard.' McGuire woke me up again. 'Clive's been in a car crash.'

The French promoter had driven Clive back from the bar in his Citroën 2CV and crashed at high speed. No seat belt, Clive went through the windscreen. His face bruised and cut, the hospital stitched, bandaged and discharged Clive to recuperate in his hotel room. We were allowed to visit, the curtains drawn and the mood sombre. His face was badly swollen; with blood clotted in tiny knots around his half-closed black eyes. He didn't look good.

'It could have been much worse,' he reasoned.

'You still have to play tonight, without Clive,' Bienkov told us. 'We need the money to pay for the trip.'

'Wendi can sing my parts,' Clive offered, 'can't you, Wendi.'
Wendi was throwing up in a sink at the time.

'Yes, all right,' she replied, unconvincingly.

Wendi wasn't capable of doing the show; she flew back to London with Clive, his stitches partially hidden by thick wrap-around sunglasses, so as not to alarm other passengers. The rest of us steeled ourselves to play our debut concert in Europe without our front man or main backing singer. We concocted a set of cover versions that McGuire could sing. Some 'special guests' sang on a couple of numbers. Fellow English rock-group, Living In Texas, happened to be at the gig and very kindly helped us out. The rest of the set was filled with the few Medics songs that the remaining backing singer, Sue, could handle; performing the two-girl choreography on her own; the dance routine of the ridiculous.

A good sport, Sue Hopkins had joined The Anadin Brothers to fill a space left by the departure of 'Old Sue' and Jane. Another Southend girl, Sue was a fan and friend of the band. Voluptuous and ample, handsome rather than pretty, she fashioned, as many punk ladies did in the 80s, Siouxsie Sioux look-alike eye make-up and a similar hairstyle. Her voice was much better than her predecessors'; she was a nice girl and game for a laugh. Sue sang on most of the bands major recordings, including the single *Miracle Of The Age*; producer Andy Partridge made a CCTV video recording of Sue recording her vocal part... topless.

'Sue's got lovely breasts,' the stiff sound engineer noticed.

Unfortunately, Sue left the band shortly after recording the first album. Tired of being bossed around by Wendi, Clive's jokes about her fluctuating weight and McGuire smelling her knickers after concerts, she quit to be replaced by Colette Appleby. But in Paris she had her moment to shine. The crowd went wild; it was Sue's finest moment.

9. Wonderland

Alice In Wonderland was a popular psychedelic-punk-Goth-rock club held on Monday nights at Gossips. Started by a tall, foundation-smeared, dress-wearing fop named Christian Paris, alongside Clive, the wacky Doctor; it filled a gap left by the previous Monday psych night (The Clinic) and was pivotal to the rise in popularity of The Medics. Between those dingy walls, the stench of stale alcohol and sweat, lengths of tattered toilet paper (sellotaped to the ceiling to disguise an empty club to early birds), plus the regular clientele of Bohemia's least fashionable misfits, Alice In Wonderland provided a focus for the alternative music scene and a sanctuary for London's outcasts, weirdoes and other social rejects. We became the unofficial house band. Doctor and the Medics played at The Clinic just once, but Alice In Wonderland gave us the opportunity to play as often as we liked, often under pseudonyms. We appeared as Gwylm & The Raspberry Flavoured Cat on the Alice In Wonderland live album *A Very Strange Way To Catch A Lobster* (on which I played a bass solo with a broken string). We also appeared under the moniker Masher Mick & The Mastic Asphalt Spreaders, and Jonathan The Tap-Dancing Giraffe & The Irritated Rug. Pseudonyms were especially useful as we became bigger, secret gigs were scheduled regularly for club anniversaries or if we needed a warm-up gig. It was on one such anniversary Alice show that my good friend Gordon The Caterpillar spiked my beer with Lysergic Acid Diethylamide.

Gordon The Caterpillar was a friend of Mr Vom, so named because his name was Gordon, and on the occasion of our first meeting he was wearing a sleeping bag fashioned to look like a caterpillar. Featuring antennae and multiple tiny legs stitched down the front that swung to and fro as he scuttled about, dragging a trail of duck-down behind him like a beer-sodden larva tail. A person with an 'individual' sense of humour but with a generous heart; on the occasion of his birthday, coinciding with an Alice's secret Medics gig, he decided to celebrate it with us. Half an hour before we were due on stage, Gordon wandered over with a bottle of lager in each hand.

'Alright, Damage,' he croaked, 'd'ya wanna beer?'

I accepted the cold beer gratefully.

'Thank you,' I said. 'Happy birthday!'

I raised the bottle to my lips to toast Gordon's special day.

46

'There's Acid in that,' he smirked, chuckling like the choked engine of an old motor bike, 'huh-huh-huh.'

'Yeah right,' I said and swigged from the bottle.

'No really, I put Acid in that bottle,' he insisted unconvincingly.

To spike someone's, anyone's, drink is very uncool. To spike a musician's drink before a performance is plain evil. I examined his eyes, searching for truth, he grinned stupidly with a dumb drunken glint, but there seemed to be no sign of malevolence.

'Nah, you didn't,' I concluded and finished the bottle.

Five minutes before stage time, backstage in the tiny nicotine-stained Gossips dressing room, the band prepared with various items of garish clothing fashioned from velvet or silk. Mr Vom bounced in and scrutinised my pupils.

'Gordon gave you Acid,' he chirped.

'No, he was joking, I'm fine,' I said as we pushed our way through the crowd that surrounded the two open sides of the small corner stage.

The band started playing, jumping and dancing, and so did the audience, loud, tight and rocking; when The Medics were on form we were awesome, and this night we ruled.

I was really enjoying the gig, the crowd were smiling and the music was solid and powerful. As we approached the midway part of the set I began to take particular pride in my musicianship, adding extra flourish and soloing within the spaces left by the other instrumentation. I was REALLY enjoying this gig and continued to solo between the songs. The segue bass-lines seemed to be popular, so, as we continued through the set, I stopped playing the bass parts entirely and just soloed throughout. I felt creative, confident and amazing; I wanted to perform the most spectacular bass playing possible, in front of this beautifully receptive audience of like-minded music lovers. I looked up from my fret-board and at Vom; he had a grin a mile wide and eyes like saucers. His neck stretched towards me, the veins vivid blue and purple. His arms seemed comparatively small and stumpy, flapping around his waist like the beating wings of an insect in flight. I looked back at my fingers; they were pink spaghetti, draped over the fingerboard of my bass which had turned to rosewood water, splashes of splintered mother of pearl licked up around my rippling knuckles.

'SHIT- I'M TRIPPING!'

Fuck, there really was LSD in that beer, Fuck, what should I do, Fuck. I looked at the audience, they were all zombies, trudging towards me with gnashing teeth and bloodied fingernails. The neck of my bass became overly long and floppy, falling from my hand like an old rope. Mr Vom realised what was happening and laughed hysterically, his eye-balls rotating wildly like cats in a washing machine.

Clive announced another song, shit, I couldn't play. Panic began to consume my frazzled brain. In a moment of hallucinogenic brilliance, I realised that I could mime to the music. I'd simply pretend to play. My mind settled, bad trip averted, I banged my hand across the strings in time to the music. BOOM-DONG-BLAMM, I'd neglected to turn my bass down. Loud thunderous bass drones swamped the music as I bashed away, oblivious to the colossal row that I was producing. The song came to an eventual end.

'Sorry,' Clive announced, 'we can't play anymore... the bass player is tripping.'
The crowd screamed with delight, a psychedelic band on psychedelic drugs... cool. They applauded enthusiastically as we left the stage. I could still hear them as I was quietly escorted through the club and home to safely dream away the rest of my Acid trip.

Gordon The Caterpillar, it transpired, who also took LSD as a special birthday treat, ended up unconscious in a puddle of piss and petrol in a multi-story car park.

10. Slang

The Medics communicated via an elaborate system of slang terminologies. Initially, between Clive, McGuire and myself, borrowed from a small black publication by Douglas Adams and John Lloyd, *'The Meaning of Liff'*. (Pan Books and Faber & Faber, 1983). A book that associated place names with verbs:

'**Wimbledon** (n): That last drop which, no matter how much you shake it, always goes down your trouser leg.'

'**Wimbledon Classic** (n): When one farts in a tennis can over a period of time, saving up the gas to form a deadly release of intestinal toxins to share with whomever a person resides.'
The later was the inspiration for the peanut butter fart jar in Clive's flat.

We confused some of the Adams and Lloyd terms:

'**Wembley** (n): The prominent stain on a man's trouser crotch, seen on his return from the lavatory (this was actually the meaning for '**Botley**'). And...
'**Wembley Proper** (n): The hideous moment of confirmation that the **Wembley** has actually struck', i.e.: pissed your pants.

Secondly, Mr Vom brought with him a peculiar Essex lingo which soon caught on with the rest of us:

Bifter (n): A booze up.

Full Bifter (n): A big booze up.

Mullered (n): Drunk.

Full Muller (n): To be very drunk whilst attending a Full Bifter.

And a twist on the traditional phrase - 'Sweet as a nut', which became - 'Sweet as a cake'.

Thirdly, Mr Vom and I adopted 'Apple and Rhyming Slang', from the TV spin-off book, *'The Goodies Files'* by Tim Brooke-Taylor, Bill Oddie and Graeme Garden, (Sphere; New Edition, 1975). By simply inserting the words 'apple and...' before other words, you appear to be speaking a kind of Cockney rhyming slang:

'Apple and stairs' - Stairs

'Apple and house' - House

'Apple and apples' - Apples. Etc.

We created our own, the most used was:

'Apple and happening'- Happening (as in an event or occurrence).
Which was abbreviated to:

'A&H'

Then we combined Apple and Happening slang with the phrase 'sweet as a cake':

'A&H as a cake.'- It is good.
Variants of which could be:

'A&H to the max.'- It is very good.

Sometimes we'd abbreviate the lot to a simple:
     '**Apple**' (n): It's all good.

In conclusion, a typical conversation between Mr Vom and myself might be...
     'I'm still mullered as a cake from last night; went for a bifter. A&H to the max- ended up as a full bifter back at my gaff. Phil Slaughter got a Wembley Proper.... ha ha ha.'
     'Apple.'

11. Glastonbury

Thrice we played at the Glastonbury festival, twice it
rained. The first time was in the middle of a run of
summer shows; we arrived at the site in fine form but
woefully unprepared for Glastonbury mud. The
Medics-mobile manoeuvred down the narrow lane
towards the entrance gate, shiny, clean and white,
whilst a stream of festival goers trolled back up, with
clothes filthy and damp; their faces daubed with soil.
The field looked like film footage, the no-man's land
of World War One, except in colour. Dark skies, loud
plosive noise with vast swathes of mottled browns
overloaded the senses... and it was wet. Tractors
heaved bogged-down vehicles from our path as we
attempted to enter; mangy dogs scuttled amongst
pallets and overturned oil drums looking for scraps of
food and shelter from the rain. A steady flow of fresh
festival goers scrambled through gaps in the perimeter
fence as others climbed over to leave for home, whilst
overstretched security men tried to prevent both. A
crew of beefy men pushed our van between flattened
tents and temporary shelters of jagged corrugated iron
as the rear wheels fought for grip. Everything was
running late, many bands were lost or had simply
turned around. We were given priority treatment.

As our crew, Martin Pyle and Alex Bienkov,
laced up walking boots that they'd sensibly brought
with them, the rest of us searched for carrier bags and
tape. I wrapped my brand new grey suede Chelsea
boots in plastic and gaffer tape ready to step out of the

van, immediately sinking to my ankles in wet, sticky brown mud. Ushered into the relative calm of the backstage area, we had a chance to survey our surroundings and its casualties. A familiar voice caught my attention, it was my friend 'John the Git', waving at me from the other side of the backstage perimeter. A skinny man who never wore socks, he was drenched; his grimy ankles protruding from two steaming clumps of cow-pat hardened mud.

'Be kind,' he shivered. 'I've taken a little Acid.'
Exhausted from cold and fatigue, his friends, tent and money lost, I took pity and smuggled him to the backstage catering tent for a paper plate of hot veggie stew and a lentil biscuit.

Playing Glastonbury feels special; the weight of rock history hangs in the air, the audience spans the generations, old hippies, young punks, spotty students and trendy grandparents; they all add to the sense of occasion and appreciate good music, new and old. We climbed the ramp behind 'The Other Stage', stepped out onto the hallowed boards, sparked up our instruments and began to play - and were immediately pelted by a barrage of thick, wet mud. Some acne-faced soap dodgers were merrily chucking mud pats at us. Smiling as they aimed, cheering as the projectiles hit a prized target, our faces (especially Clive's) or our guitars, the strings were clagging with mud. Stage crew frantically taped plastic sheeting over our expensive equipment (a particularly large mud missile ruined my Trace Elliot speaker, the magnetic coil splattered and the paper cone saturated). Clive's hair was matted, his best threads spoilt, he shot his hand into the air, caught a fresh clump of just-launched mud and hurled it back into the front row. It hit the face of a smirking kid with a smack that miraculously coincided with the start of McGuire's guitar solo. Clive dropped his microphone and leapt from the stage, over the security moat, landing at the feet of the astonished boy then punched him square in the face; his fist heavy with large silver rings. Martin Pyle jumped down behind Clive to help him back onto stage - just in time to pick up his microphone and finish the song.

'Fucking bastard,' the punched boy screamed at Clive.

Martin plucked the boy's spectacles from his nose, snapped them in half, threw them to the ground and stamped them into the dirt. The rest of us watched helplessly, unable to warn Clive or Martin that they'd just beaten up the wrong person, an innocent fan who wasn't throwing mud. The guilty perpetrators stopped immediately.

The gig was considered a great success; we'd played to a lot of people, and the mud on our amps was 'mystical Glastonbury mud' according to Wendi, therefore magical and brilliant. Backstage, Mr Vom entertained with a few rounds of 'kamikaze snakebite', gulping the local scrumpy and 'shot gunning' cans of lager. Some friends and liggers managed to sneak backstage and turned the dressing room tent into a party event. One of these liggers was a skateboarding punk who we'd met a few weeks previously at a gig in Redcar. He was tripping on psilocybin mushrooms and wanted to share the experience.

'The plants are trying to tell us something,' he said cryptically.

I thought it might be fun to take a few magic mushrooms in the van on the way home; the roads in the West Country were very green, and there would be lots on things to view from the window during the long journey. The Anadin Brothers agreed, as did McGuire and Mr Vom. The skateboarding punk looked directly in my eyes.

'I would be honoured to venture forth with you, to find mushrooms,' he offered sincerely, 'you have true and worthy eyes.'
I turned down his kind offer; he was scary.

A tractor dragged our van through the muddy swamp towards the exit, we trudged behind; my grey suede Chelsea boots were ruined, but a small bag of magic mushrooms was stashed safely in my pocket (another friend, Sandra from Gossips, had secured a batch before we left). We waited for stragglers; I leant against a fence post to untangle the filthy plastic and gaffer tape wrapping from my feet whilst I considered a dappled green shape that was marching steadily towards me through the mud. I squinted at the khaki blob, trying to pick out any distinguishing features. As the object approached, a hand appeared and unzipped a small section from the top of its body - it was a hood.

'Alright,' it said.
The brother of John the Git, David, had climbed the Glastonbury fence wearing his army-surplus sleeping bag parka. He unzipped the entire shit smeared garment and showed off its genius functionality. It kept him dry when it rained; he could sleep in it, so didn't need to carry or pitch a tent.

'I can sleep where I fall,' he announced proudly.
He'd taken Acid also.

The long journey home was made much worse by Clive.

'Regretting taking magic mushrooms, are we?' he wise-cracked, as we each suffered our individual torments. Hallucinogenic drugs are really not compatible with busy and dangerous motorways. The green West Country scenery (smiling sheep, waving trees and sea-spray pastures) was soon replaced by mile upon mile of grey oppressive concrete, and I couldn't work out if my imagination was playing tricks or whether I urgently needed a piss.

12. The Way Up

We first met Andrew King at The Escape Club in
Brighton. He was drunk. He'd driven down from
London to check us out; he liked what he saw and told
us so and then drove back again, drunk. He was an
old-school music manager with a public school accent.
Often sporting a crumpled linen suit with Hush
Puppies and bifocals, he carried about him the
deportment of assumed grandeur that only comes with
worldly experience, upper-class confidence and the
over-consumption of Gordon's Gin. In the swinging
sixties he'd managed Pink Floyd with his business
partner Peter Jenner. When Syd Barrett left the group,
Andrew King stayed with Syd to help manage his solo
career fade into rock oblivion. Peter Jenner continued
to work with Pink Floyd and made millions. Andrew

had dealt with Marc Bolan, unsuccessfully, turned down David Bowie (considering him untalented) and appeared emptying a box of dead butterflies into the crowd at Hyde Park during the film of the famous Rolling Stones concert. He could name-drop for England, and we were suitably impressed. Previously, he had managed Dickensian rock legends Ian Dury and The Blockheads and bouffant songstress Mari Wilson; he liked hard-working live acts, and we ticked his boxes. With a new business partner, the lipstick addicted ginger-haired Diddy-woman Jenny Cotton, Andrew touted us around the record labels and publishing houses of eighties London.

Armed with new demo recordings produced by Roman Jug (at Elephant Studios in Wapping) and some glossy photos, which became known as the Vom pineapple head shoot (so called because Mr Vom's new hair cut resembled a pineapple), Andrew was confident that he could sign us to a major label. We had by now received our first review in the music press, a small piece on the first Alice In Wonderland Film Festival at The Scala Cinema in Kings Cross (The Medics played live between sixties cult movies). There was also a 'live' record with which to impress record executives. The *Live at Alice In Wonderland EP*, again produced by Roman Jug, a 4-track studio recording of some of our live set, including *She Sells Flowers By Candlelight* and a cover of The Sweet classic *Blockbuster*, all with fake crowd noise mixed underneath. Listeners with keen ears could hear us chanting 'Medics Medics', and 'fatty fatty', over a U2 live-album crowd - to create the illusion of an audience and bring attention to McGuire's portliness. It wasn't very convincing but was fun to sell at gigs. We also had a cheap video made for our song *The Goats Are Trying To Kill Me,* filmed in a local Scout hut. Well-known on the live scene and constantly gigging, we too were sure that our posh manager would soon manage us a nice fat record deal. He didn't.

One day Andrew called Clive, McGuire and myself into a quiet room after the sound-check at a college gig. In hushed tones he explained that he'd approached every major record label in the country, and none of them were interested, with one exception. IRS Records (owned by Miles Copeland, brother of the drummer in new wave band The Police) were prepared to sign us to an unimpressive development deal. He advised that we should accept the offer and then left with some of our drinks rider. We told Mr Vom and the girls the news.

Despite Andrew's obvious disappointment that it wasn't a big money record deal, it was still a record deal, and as such we were excited. IRS had such artists as:

Hairy Welsh acoustic strummers - The Alarm.

Glam-Goth stoners - Lords Of The New Church. And Mr Vom's favourite band of all time - The Cramps. Finally, we thought, we were on the way up.

We were to sign both our music and publishing away to IRS; a lawyer explained that even though the money was bad, we were less likely to be dropped by a 'smaller' label - which was a good thing.

We were plied with champagne as we signed the contracts in the IRS building and were invited (along with Andrew King, Jenny Cotton, full road crew, plus various music journalists and A&R staff) for a slap-up curry in the afternoon sitting at Khan's restaurant in Kensington. We were still there as the evening customers arrived. Mr Vom and I sat at the far end and ordered everything on the menu, literally. When there wasn't room on the table, we'd hide the steaming dishes between the table legs. As the waiters fetched fresh lager we ordered more. Free beer and curry, this was the life. But, when a music journo was asked to make a speech, he gave us some earth-shattering news.

'There's no such thing as a free lunch.' All this wasted food and drink, plus everything else for which the label writes a cheque, is recoupable; we'd have to pay the money back. A sobering thought.

IRS put us straight in a studio to record more current demos - which went very well, we always made great demo recordings. Of these demos, tracks were chosen for our first release, a five-track 12-inch EP *Auntie Evils Dormitory, Round And Round, The Mole Catchers Boot* and a cover version of Hawkwind's *Silver Machine*; each re-recorded with title track *Happy But Twisted* at The Workhouse Studios in The Old Kent Road by engineer Pete Hammond (who later became the Stock Aitken Waterman in-house re-mixer). Released in 1985 through Illegal Records (the independent side label of IRS), the record was played by Radio One champion John Peel and went to number two in the UK indie charts.

Next up was *The Miracle Of The Age*, recorded in Peter Gabriel's Real World 1 Studios in Bath, produced by Andy Partridge, leader of the thinking man's-punk outfit XTC. Andy re-worked the song into a back-beat soul stomper that never felt good when we rehearsed, played or recorded it but suited his production style. He was good company; a man with simple tastes, he liked his real-ale and taught us a lot about the recording process. I drew a cartoon of him holding a rubber shark (featured on the back of the record sleeve; the shark was a masturbatory device favoured on tour by certain members of XTC). Also released in 1985, this second single, although interesting and released through IRS proper, didn't chart. The mix suffered from lack of studio time, Andy was fatigued and malnourished, Wendi having insisted that we ate her 'all natural' home-made nut curry, which he naturally hated.

American producer Craig Leon was chosen to produce our debut album. He'd previously worked on the first Ramones and Blondie albums. We liked these records - they were pop-rock-classics. He was a small, round man with a dark complexion and demonic goatee facial hair that made him look like a character from The Addams Family. Assisted by his girlfriend and sixties rock-chic, Cassell Webb, they entertained us with anecdotes of Moroccan opiates, wild sixties abandon and classic New York rock'n'roll. We hoped our album would reflect these passions; however, it turned out limp and lacklustre, not a pop-rock classic at all.

Initially we were pleased with the album, often the case when you're used to hearing it loud in a studio. It featured such material as *Barbara Can't Dance*, *Lucky Lord Jim* and *Kettle On A Long Chain*. Miles Copeland and some of his colleagues from MCA (a major label with whom IRS had negotiated distribution) arrived on the last day of the recording session (at Britannia Row Studios in Islington) for an album 'play-back'. The record industry types sat in the control room with Clive and some lager, whilst Craig Leon turned the volume up to 10 and blasted out the album in its entirety. The rest of us played pinball in another room. Miles Copland was not happy. Unbeknownst to us, Copeland had been reprimanded by MCA for bad label sales, he used our album play-back as an opportunity to repair his losses with MCA, to save face in front of his superiors. When the last track had finished and a few A&R types finished whooping and clapping, Copeland walked to the front of the control room and addressed Craig Leon and Clive.

'I don't hear any hits,' he said. 'I'm not releasing this album unless I hear a hit record.' Embarrassed by Copeland's music-business politics but very aware of the industry machinery required to make a record a hit, Craig answered calmly...

'If I record you a hit record, as you ask, will you guarantee that you will do everything necessary to make it a hit?'
This taunted Copeland in front of the MCA big-wigs, he answered...

'Yes.'

Two days later Andrew King phoned us individually.
'We're recording a hit record... *Spirit In The Sky.*'

13. Italy

'Who iz zis leetle bouy?' The Italian police chief
insisted as he questioned McGuire; the eldest in
appearance, he was singled out for first interrogation.
Martin Pyle and I sat outside in a cool marble hallway
on a hard wooden seat, guarded by two other armed
polizia; arrested for eating crisps within an hour of our
arrival in Italy. This was a destination of desire; the
food, the wine, the girls, Italy was for us the nation of
everything delicious. We loved the place - but they
didn't like the look of us.

Our first Italian tour was great. The promoter,
keen to impress, booked us into small venues for more
money than he could afford or was likely to make from
ticket sales. His logic being that on our second Italian
tour he would book into larger venues and charge
more for tickets, recoup any losses and make a healthy
profit (this is the template for how music promoters
work). His plan was unfortunately compromised by
the ridiculous cost of our consumption of food and
drink. After every sound-check we were whisked away
by an amiable Italian translator for a fantastic meal in
top restaurants, where we ate and drank vast quantities
of everything. The translator was happy to pick up the
bill for the oblivious promoter, who never saw these
restaurant costs until it was too late, and he had
already lost a small fortune. On our second tour he
cunningly employed a sarcastic expatriated Scouser to
guard us and the purse strings. Who kept a tight grip
on every expense and put a stop to all wasteful

mischief. But the initial tour was a feed fest, a quest to experience every scrumptious Italian delicacy, antipasti, speciality meat and the chef's recommended dish. We were ravenous and ruinous, rivalled only by our thirst for fine wine, beer and the local 120 proof Grappa.

On arrival in this land of plenty, impressed with the hotel that the generous promoter had provided, fresh from a pleasant flight and keen to explore, three of us decided to wander around the quiet Bologna streets, curious and peckish. Everything was shut save for a tiny cubical selling magazines, cigarettes and potato crisps. New to the novelty of European snacks we each purchased a large bag of exotic flavoured crisps and roamed the deserted roads munching as we walked. We came upon a solitary street bench and sat to finish our light lunch, chatting quietly and enjoying the scenery. A few minutes passed before a police siren suddenly broke the sleepy atmosphere, shrill, urgent and loud, accompanied by the scream of braking car tyres. A police car screeched to a halt, three fierce policemen sprang out and shouted at us in a foreign language, surrounding our bench whilst fingering machine guns buckled to their hips.

'Passportz,' they yelled.

They snatched away our passports as we offered them for inspection. Without looking at our documents they bundled us into the rear of the police car, our bags of crisps confiscated and unfinished. We sat speechless, confused and terrified as the vehicle tore through the streets at death-defying speed, siren on. In moments, we arrived at the steps of an oppressive square building which we correctly assumed was the police station. We were pulled from the vehicle, up the steps and through the reception area and rudely shoved onto a bench outside the chief policeman's office door. McGuire was pushed into the office; he looked back at me as the heavy door was shut behind him, his eyes swollen and scared. We strained our ears as McGuire was scrutinised about our suspicious activities and curious documents.

'Who iz zis leetle bouy?'

My passport photo was taken when I was just fourteen; the police hadn't checked my updated photograph a few pages later, he demanded to know why we were in possession of a child's passport and the location of this young boy.

The Italian authorities eventually released us after failing to maintain who we were or what we were doing in their country.

'You do not know ze name of your employer?'

McGuire couldn't explain that we were musicians, or why musicians don't carry employment documents. The irate police threw us out onto the street to find out own way back to the hotel, without explanation and without returning our crisps.

14. The Dock

Our first televised appearance was on a programme called 'Rock At The Dock'. Filmed at a studio in Docklands, each episode featured a different contemporary band, playing a 60 minute live set to a captive TV audience - rocking at the dock. We were invited through our association with The Damned, who were filmed for the show several days before; Roman to make a guest appearance during our final song as part of the deal. On arrival, we were mightily impressed; the studio was huge and the sound system substantial, with a massive lighting rig constructed over and around the large three-tiered stage, surrounded by proper television cameras - the type that cameramen could sit on.

The sound-check was followed by a complete run-through of our live set; the cameramen practiced shots, the director his angles, and we performed like it was an actual gig. The producer loved us. Each band member had their own cameraman, filming Mr Vom through his kit and over his head, close-ups of McGuire's finger-work and Clive's body contortions. Lots of attention was paid to the Anadin Brothers' choreography and crash-zoom point of view angles up their skirts. My cameraman liked to film through my legs, chasing me around as I hopped up and down between the tiered stages, he said that we should do that again during the actual filming.

Once we'd changed into our finest stage gear and the make-up ladies had daubed various foundations and powders to our faces, applied black lipstick to Mr Vom's mouth (curiously at his request) and wished us good luck, we prepared to resume our places on stage. We were introduced onto the stage by boomy-voiced rock DJ Tommy Vance. The audience hadn't heard of us but cheered dutifully, and then we were on; lights-camera-action.

We exploded into our well-practiced and sonically honed performance, thick power chords, big drum rolls, fast bass riffs, garage punk vocals with screeching harmonies. Our respective cameramen crouched and darted, re-capturing their best shots from our earlier run-through. The first song finished, and Clive saluted to the crowd.

'Thank you, Rock At The Dock,' he said in his exaggerated US drawl.

Canned audience applause blasted from the speaker, the small audience were drowned-out and confused by the eruption of pre-recorded enthusiasm. My nerves subsided; I relaxed into the performance and began skipping back and forth between the stepped stages as the cameraman chased me for his signature 'between the leg' shot. This would be the first time that I fell over on stage. I lost balance in my Cuban-heeled Chelsea boots, tripped over the camera, tumbled and ripped my tight paisley ankle-swinger hipster trousers across both knees. The cameraman captured the event in its entirety, including my stupid grin and blushing cheeks as I scrambled to my feet and tried to pretend that nothing had happened. I was assured after the filming that this embarrassing moment would be edited out of the final programme.

The set was a triumph, before we knew it we'd reached our final song and were blasting through frantic drum-roll crescendo solo-wankery, the cliché big rock ending that most bands succumb to at one time or another. As the last chords were strummed, bashed and plonked, Mr Vom twirled his sticks, and I swung my metallic purple bass by the guitar strap in a pendulum arch around my shoulders. Mr Vom smashed a final cymbal, Clive scissor kicked into the air, and the cameras stopped rolling, just in time to miss the headstock of my custom bass crash against the edge of the stage, snap and shatter into a cascade of splintered mahogany and glitter paint.

After the performance, flushed with post-gig adrenalin and hospitality alcohol, we were permitted to watch the rushes of the footage in an editing room. It looked really good, lots of energy and high octane fun. Mr Vom looked particularly good, the camera flying round his head, sticks cutting the air, muscles rippling with his black lipstick outlining his hobgoblin punk rock star smile. Andrew King explained that drummers always come out well on TV; lots of movement and easy to film, because they stay in one place.

When the program was finally aired, I discovered to my horror that the director hadn't edited out my embarrassment but repeated the shot of me falling over, in slow motion, twice.

15. Crew

'Always remember the road crew,' once remarked the legendary Motörhead front man Lemmy Kilmister; these are wise words. Crew members swap and change, they may start as van drivers then progress to roadie or tour manager, or may simply be a man with a van and are happy to stay that way. But whether they are TMs, stage techs, light riggers or soundmen you need to be friends, you can spend a lot of time together. Binky, Pyley, Harry D'mac, Johnny Prism, Fartus Bartus, Secret Squirrel, Josh, Welsh Carl, Chief, Bazza Gorman, Spunky, Jeff the Rage, Andy Veg and several others, all these road-hardened technicians worked with The Medics and were, mostly, our great mates.

Van driver, roadie and, at various times over the years, tour manager, Martin Pyle (another Eltham Scout) saved my life once, in France. A weekend music festival in Rennes at which we shared a stage with bouncy fifties boppers Buddy Curtess And The Grasshoppers, Gothic lovely Danielle Dax and pub-punk rockers Screaming Blue Messiahs, all up for it and all drunk on delicious Fischer beer. After a successful gig and post stage jolly-up we returned to our hotel; a grand building with an impressive staircase that rose up from the ground floor throughout the many levels in a big white wooden spiral. Everyone retired to their rooms apart from Mr Vom and I, talking shit in bad French accents, sharing a last bottle of continental lager whilst leaning against the stairs. As we drained the back-wash, a door opened, Clive sprinted out, picked me up by the armpits and threw me half over the stairwell banister. I objected as best I could and grabbed the banister with both hands.

'Zoot allor,' I exclaimed.

Mr Vom continued our dialogue.

'Ahh, Monsieur D'mage you appeer to hev fellen over le' stairs,' he retorted observantly.

Now, there is one thing about Mr Vom that is a given fact; he means no malice, but he will join in with any mischievous shenanigans when drunk. As I hung precariously over the stairwell, my knees hooked over the banister, the wacky Doctor said to Mr Vom;

'Grab his legs!'

Clive pulled one ankle up and outwards; Mr Vom obliged and worked on the other. I slipped further backwards, my fingers gripping tighter around the slippery, varnished banister rail, the sinews in my arm strained and taut.

'Meard,' I managed, as I pressed against the rail with my remaining leg.

'Bite his hands, Vom,' Clive instructed.

Mr Vom chewed my fingers, tormenting the joints with a succession of fast sharp nibbles. The seriousness of the situation began to sober me up; I noticed the glint of villainous intent in Clive's eyes, laughing hysterically as my spine inched ever downwards.

'Fuck, you're gonna break my neck,' I realised out loud, in English.

'Take your shoe off, Vom,' Clive ordered, 'hit his knuckles.'

Mr Vom obediently removed his creeper and started hammering down upon my white clenched knuckles, the skin discolouring into a moody purple from the blows. Clive tried to wrench my other hand from the rail, jabbing my wrist to weaken my hold.

'That's it, Vom,' he laughed, levering my grip free, one finger at a time.

In a flash of clarity and horror, I saw the method to this act of madness, Clive's evil genius, this attempted manslaughter. If/when I fell, I would break my back, neck, skull or all three. The band would get publicity from the terrible rock'n'roll tragedy; infamy and notoriety would inevitably follow, Clive's fortune would be made; fame at any cost. If there were criminal charges pressed, Clive would blame Vom, it was he, after all, who was walloping my bruised knuckles with his blue suede brothel creeper.

Sheer terror filled every cell of my body; I was going to die. I filled my lungs full of French air, opened my mouth and screamed. Mr Vom briefly stopped his barrage of blows, momentarily startled by the sound of genuine fear in my voice. I yelled as loudly as I could. Clive continued to pummel my aching wrists with added urgency.

'Quick Vom,' he shouted, 'just a little bit more.'

Out from the nowhere appeared two muscular arms, they forced between the two would-be assassins and threw them aside. It was Martin Pyle, he grabbed the collar of my jacket with one hand and pulled me from my spirally hell; his other fist fending off a renewed last minute attack. He pushed me into my hotel room and slammed the door behind.

'Lock this fucking door,' he shouted.

Saving the bass player's life isn't on the work description for most tour managers, but if it were, Martin performed that duty admirably.

16. Hype

We were not too happy with producer Craig Leon's suggestion to record *Spirit In The Sky*. We obviously knew the 1969 original, written and recorded by moustachioed coffee-house long-hair Norman Greenbaum - it is a truly fantastic record. We just didn't like the lyric...

'I've got a friend in Jesus.'

Songs about Christianity were not considered very cool, not in keeping with our street credibility; songs about Jesus were just not rock'n'roll. We were summoned round to Craig Leon's house to discuss the matter.

Craig's place, which he shared with partner Cassell Webb, was a spacious and plush studio apartment, equipped with a substantial record collection as well as several bookshelves full with all things mysterious and mystical. Hardbound volumes about cosmology, astronomy, theology, escapology and Egyptology. Paperbacks on theoretical, practical and particle physics, quasi-religious and occultists pamphlets on paganism and dualism - it was fair to say he had some subject matter to hand. He convinced us that the 'spirit in the sky' was in fact the astrological sign of Orion, revered throughout pagan history as The Hunter, but utilised by early Christianity as John The Baptist, a 'friend of Jesus'. Baffled by pseudo-science, we chose to believe him and agreed to record the song. The 'hit record', someone else's 'hit record' that Miles Copeland had insisted on.

The recording process was successful and quick. The lush string arrangement was skilfully orchestrated by Craig Leon on a heavy studio synthesiser keyboard called a Kurzweil, as were most of the other instruments. Clive double-tracked his vocals with a soft, Marc Bolan-esque whisper to help disguise his Elvis meets Dave Vanian impression. Wendi and Sue Hopkins (shortly to quit), assisted by Cassell Webb, sang the backing parts accurately. It sounded good, but other than the strings, Clive's flat vocal in the first verse, and the slightly stiff groove compared to the original, the finished recording was a part by part copy of the Norman Greenbaum record. IRS were happy.

We'd done our bit, now it was the record label's turn. As promised by Miles Copeland at the album playback, the cogs of the music industry were oiled; the machinery of the record business was put in motion. The record sleeve, with the strap-line 'the six-track sell-out pack' featured a pull-out double-sided poster of the band and limited edition live recordings, as well as the B-side *Laughing At The Pieces* (the title track of the debut album that was inexplicably cut from the final running order). Clive was booked on an extensive schedule of radio and television interviews to promote the single, including 'The Tube' with Glaswegian trendy Muriel Grey, and 'TV-AM' with Lady Diana wannabe Selina Scott. Radio DJs and producers, the powerful behind-the-scenes people who choose the playlists, were bribed with bottles of 'Medics Spirit' (*Spirit In The Sky* labels specially printed and stuck over bottles of cheap Scotch). The best radio plugger money could buy, a tall hand-shaking Jewish gentleman named Oliver Smallman, knew who to charm and did it well. The first radio play was by Radio One DJ and Cliff Richard look-alike Mike Reed, closely followed and championed by bubbly northerner Bruno Bookes.

We resented having to record *Spirit In The Sky*; we didn't like it - that was until we heard it on the radio. It sounded good. It sounded like 'a hit'.

17. Paddling

One night, in Germany, Mr Vom handed me a can of beer, a type that I'd never seen before, 'Whiskey Beer'. Martin Pyle had one as well, he'd found a small stock of them in our dressing room fridge. It was horrible, cheap, acidic whisky blended with nasty sour beer, it tasted like a dog had just vomited into your mouth. Martin, however, quite liked it - he drank lots.

The following morning, we were woken by a relentless banging on our door; it was Martin.

'Quick, get up; we're leaving in ten minutes.'

We were staying in a beautiful scenic ski-lodge style hotel, run by a friendly lady, who very kindly extended our check-out time by an hour from 10 until 11am. We could hear her cleaning rooms around us. Martin was insistent that we were in the van, ready to leave, at 11am precisely, not a second later; it was already 10.45.

We scrambled ourselves together, slowly, confused by the rush. We didn't have to be anywhere else in a hurry, it was a rest day; nothing but a leisurely drive to the next gig location.

'Quickly, quickly,' Martin dragged us from our room. 'We're leaving right now.' It was 10.50am.

'What's the rush?' Mr Vom asked, deliberately taking his time, fiddling with the key in the lock.

The cleaning lady smiled politely and pushed her trolley of soaps, towels and cleaning products towards Martin's room.

'No! I still haven't quite got everything out yet; do these boys' room first. They've checked out,' Martin snapped, blocking his doorway. The lady dutifully entered our room.

'Look.' Martin opened his door slightly ajar for us to peek inside. 'This is why we need to leave right now.'

Martin's bed looked like a duck pond; the sheets, the blankets and the pillows, all swimming in a dirty yellow-brownish liquid - with green bits floating in it. The mattress was ruined.

'I finished all of that Whiskey Beer... and wet the bed,' he said ashamedly.

'That's piss?' We couldn't believe our eyes. It looked like there was some kind of animal life growing in it - the Thing from the piss lagoon.

'Please,' Martin begged, 'let's be gone before she sees this.' He was so embarrassed.

We walked from the hotel, as calmly as we could manage and climbed into the van; the engine already running. As we pulled away we heard an ear-piercing shriek, a scream of disgust and unbridled horror; the poor lady had discovered the bed and the revolting, slimy, un-Godly swamp of stinking whiskey urine.

From this moment, thanks to Martin's nocturnal shame, we acquired a new slang term, one which we used from that morning onwards:

Paddling (n): To wet the bed whilst on tour.

18. Stupid

The stupidest thing that I ever wore was a pink crushed velvet one-piece catsuit with flared trousers and a sequined collar with matching trim. Open down to the hips to display my bare chest, stomach and a hint of pubic hair. My girlfriend Madeline made it, it made her laugh. Madeline (Mads) made most of my shirts, all of them loud, frilly and silly. Silk, satin, glittery creations that you couldn't buy in any shop, no matter how over the top its reputation; she later admitted that she wanted me to look ridiculous, to prevent the attention of groupies. McGuire asked Mads to make him a shirt once, made from sheer nylon, it was completely see-through. He conveniently lost it in a bar in Greenwich.

Wendi from the Anadin Brothers made Clive's clothes, as well as catering for the girls and a few bits for McGuire, but my stage clothes were the product of Mads and my mum. My mother made most of my sparkly, paisley or crushed velvet loons with matching waistcoats, often colour matched to Madeline's shirts. Hours spent in fabric shops searching for the craziest cloth meant that I had the least tasteful clobber possible. Mr Vom always managed to look cool, creating his own glam-punk image, matching embroidered waistcoats with PVC pants; he utilised enough hippy aesthetic to pacify the fashion code enforcers of the band, alongside the studded rock'n'roller chic of his peers. Mr Vom never looked stupid.

Band videos were always the perfect vehicle to show off your latest and loudest stage threads. My pink velvet catsuit made an appearance for a later single video called *More*, but for our first proper video, *Spirit In The Sky*, Madeline made me a shiny silver blouse that looked like it was made of BacoFoil. Coordinated with a silver-threaded blue and pink two-piece paisley ensemble, courtesy of my mother's sewing machine - I naturally thought that I looked the business.

In the 80s a video could make or break a band, *Spirit In The Sky* helped break The Medics. Come the day of filming, our morning call time was, as is always the case, very early indeed. Tired and irritated by this rude am start, we arrived sleepy and grumpy at the studio, a converted church. Plied with bacon rolls and hot tea from the assistant director, we slowly woke up as we watched the art department construct the stage set. Reminiscent of the *Miracle Of The Age* single sleeve, psychedelic wavy lines creating a three-dimensional optical illusion, an effect that was slightly pop art and very weird. We loved it immediately.

Once we'd donned our respective outfits, wigs, make-up and beads, finished lacquering, back-combing, crimping and tousling our hair, we were ready for video action. There were two main camera set-ups. A basic performance to camera, firstly just the band, with individual close-ups, then the girls. It was the first time we'd actually watched what the girls were doing. We were impressed by their simple and quirky dance routine; a haughty blend of the Egyptian sand dance and Jane Fonda aerobics, they were applauded when they finished.

The second part of the video was a parody of the kitsch 60s Batman TV show. Clive pulled himself along a horizontal rope (up the side of a fake apartment block) as we stuck our heads from windows. As on Batman, the camera filmed sideways, the final shot showing him apparently walking up a vertical wall. Inter-cut with a little stock footage of an Apollo rocket launch and a speeding shot of Clive pretending to fall backwards, the finished video was cheap and cheerful but looked fresh and fun. It was shown on the ITV 'Chart Show' and reviewed on BBCs 'Saturday Superstore' by tartan-suited heartthrob Paul King and toothy consumer television personality Esther Rantzen; they both liked it.

19. Curse

For a rock group to 'make it', to 'break through', will require an unfaltering self-belief, a total, unquestionable conviction that you are destined to succeed despite all the odds. You need blind faith. If you don't feel fated to be a pop star then chances are you probably won't be, the hunger that can only be satisfied by performing is the driving force that fuels success. To take the blows, to suffer the knocks, to take two steps backwards only to take yet another pace back, must be experienced. This is how it was with The Medics; we never saw problems as a hindrance, they were, in our eyes, clarification of our goal, mystical signposts to keep true to our quest - our guiding spirits contacting us from the musical ether.

During the recording of *Miracle Of The Age,* Andy Partridge wanted to do an edit in the middle-eight section. It was long before the days of digital recording, the studio engineer had to carefully slice the 24-track two-inch iron oxide tape with a razor blade then rejoin the ends; which he did successfully. This process was an everyday, simple and straightforward procedure that recording engineers did frequently without problem or hitch; but not with The Medics. After several hours of work (and surreptitious videotaping of Sue Hopkins tits) the engineer noticed a glitch. Andy Partridge heard it next; almost inaudible to our ears; we too eventually heard the mysterious clicking noise, just before the middle-eight. The meticulous engineer spooled the tape slowly back and forth until he located the offending sound, it was his edit point; the bonding tape used to join the two cut edges of the two-inch tape had slipped.

'I have never known this to happen or heard of this happening, in all my years as a recording engineer,' he assured us as he laboured to slice micro-millimetres of tape from the edit point and re-join the seam.

As Andy Partridge paced the room, fretting away the time that it took to repair the edit, worried for the hours of expensive studio time potentially lost, we weren't bothered. Wendi was the first to say it, but we all thought the same thing, it was The Curse of the Medics; a ghost in the machine; the mischievous phantoms of rock having a little harmless fun and more justification that we were on the right path.

The Curse of the Medics was also, so we reasoned, responsible for Clive's car crash in Paris, (what didn't kill him made us stronger and strengthened our resolve). The Curse would be cited every time the van broke down or a PA system had an electrical fault. If a ferry was late or a flight delayed, when a light bulb blew, when the stage collapsed during our 'E.C.T.' TV performance, when we got arrested before the Batcave gig, when Clive knocked himself unconscious jumping from the stage of the Marquee in Wardour St, when a lighting stack was knocked over by the audience filming 'The Old Grey Whistle Test', when a heavy lamp fell from a lighting rig almost crushing Mr Vom at the Croydon Cartoon Club.

The Curse of the Medics was our lucky charm, our karma. We were fated for greatness, in this we believed, wholeheartedly.

20. Television

Since appearing on 'Rock At The Dock', we'd had varying degrees of luck with television. To promote the *Happy But Twisted* EP we'd played on a new Rock TV show called 'E.C.T.', alongside female metal band Rock Goddess and plump pub-rockers Dumpy's Rusty Nuts. The two number set featuring *The Molecatcher's Boot* and *Silver Machine* came across well, despite the stage collapsing during live filming - looking and sounding good on the telly box.

Whilst on tour to promote the single *Miracle Of The Age* we were invited to perform on the influential BBC2 late night music programme 'The Old Grey Whistle Test'. A fantastic programme that we all watched and admired. Since we were touring, it was decided that we'd be filmed with our audience on an 'Outside Broadcast' live from the Bristol Bierkeller; introduced by left-field boozer Andy Kershaw. I was far too exited during the sound-check, fidgety and nervous. I decided to change my bass strings even though I didn't need to - big mistake. I'd usually over-tighten new strings, to stretch out any slack to keep them in better tune. But this time, as I wound the second fattest (A) string, I stupidly over-tightened it, and it snapped. I had another, and re-strung my bass as the band continued to sound-check I broke that string as well, my last spare. Trembling with nerves, I tried over-tightening the fattest (E) string to tune to (A), the neck of my bass bent like a boomerang. Eyes burning with alarm and utter panic, I sprinted around Bristol looking for a music shop, whilst the rest of the band rehearsed for the director and film crew without me.

The gig was great but a terrible disappointment when I watched a video recording of the programme. The bass guitar was barely audible (because I hadn't sound-checked). The sound director didn't realise that there should have been a bass player in the mix as well. A couple of months afterwards a Glaswegian drunkard came up to me in my local pub.

'Here Pal, how comes your band's shit!?' he asked with an air of violent menace.
McGuire was sitting next to me, the drunkard didn't notice him, so he sat bravely silent.

'I saw you on Whistle Test, ya were shit,' he said.

A TV documentary crew following Miles Copeland, making a programme about the music industry, filmed some scenes at one of our concerts. The London School of Economics, it was a decent size venue and very full. Our A&R man, shoe fetishist Steve Tannett, got to 'big-up' the band on camera.

'My band play to 1000 kids a night,' he exaggerated.

The director wanted to film Copeland and the band chatting in the dressing room before the gig. We thought it hilarious to cross and re-cross our legs every time that Clive coughed. We flicked our legs back and forth like can-can dancers throughout the interview, synchronised and ridiculous; Copeland wasn't happy.

'Fetch the release papers,' he hissed when the camera crew left the room.

His girlfriend was entertaining though; California-tanned, gym-fit with sexy curves but dim, she thought McGuire's guitar was made from a pair of old pink paisley pyjamas... and showed genuine concern for Clive's nasty cough.

Doctor and the Medics would perform on many great British TV shows like Channel 4's flagship show 'The Tube', as well as lesser ones including 'Razzamatazz', presented by beak-nosed diva Lisa Stansfield, 'Number 73', with a set that resembled a day-glow crack-den, and the excruciatingly embarrassing children's game show 'Cheggers Plays Pop', presented by professional knob Keith Chegwin. But the pinnacle of any aspiring musician was to appear on the ultimate music television programme, perhaps the greatest television programme ever, 'Top Of The Pops', and we did it five times, including the Christmas special.

The first time, we arrived late; they'd already started camera rehearsals, and the affronted director was about to replace us with another group. On the first rehearsal there was nothing to direct other than a lonely drum kit and a microphone stand. Jenny Cotton was flapping around the BBC Shepherds Bush TV Centre reception, skipping about like she'd wet her knickers. She rushed us through to the studio just in time for the second run-through of *Spirit In The Sky* without guitars. We felt like total idiots, but at least we were there. We had a chance to strap on our guitars for the final run-through and could relax into the day.

Pre-show drinks in the BBC bar were part of the ritual, according to Andrew King; a cheap, post-lunch drinky, shared with the other bands on the show, with the opportunity to ogle one of the Benny Hill Show girls or rub shoulders with a Blue Peter presenter. Mr Vom larked around with the drummers from over-hyped hairdressers Sigue Sigue Sputnik, but it seemed fairly tame, and we felt bloated from a celebrity spotting nosh-up in the BBC canteen.

After another couple of camera runs, this time in full stage gear, we were led into the make-up department and then back on stage for the filming of the show. The studio was surprisingly small; an excited crowd of Sunday-best dressed teenagers were herded between heavy television cameras, noisily dashing between stages alternately; their chance to meet a pop star, to glimpse someone famous. Each act had its own stage from several positioned around the edges of the studio, the audience clapped dutifully as canned applause boomed through the sound system - louder than the bands. We were introduced by Radio 1 DJ Simon Bates and silently counted in by the floor manager's fingers:

> four...
> three...
> two...
> one.

Nerves and ego were channelled into a three minute performance, one which we'd rehearsed and imagined since child hood. We mimed energetically to a barely audible backing track, humming along to our parts to keep time, trying not to watch ourselves on the huge overhead monitor screens (the reason that bands often seem to be looking up instead of at the audience). The music faded quickly, the cameras and crowd chased off to the next stage. It was over.

'What happened, why didn't you sing?' our bemused plugger, Oliver Smallman, asked the girls as we celebrated back in the dressing room.

'I'm not fucking miming on fucking 'Top Of The fucking Pops',' fumed Wendi, her eyes fiery with rage and Sandeman Port.

Throughout our performance, on every single shot of the girls, the camera crew had expertly captured The Anadin Brothers, perfectly lit and shot from many angles, performing the extensive vocal arrangement and quirky dance routine...with mouths tightly shut.

21. Out the window

It's good to have a hobby, especially one that keeps the mind active or the body fit, but Mr Vom's favourite sporting activity was neither. He called it 'out the window' because it involved, as the name accurately suggests, jumping out of windows. He enjoyed it greatly.

The rules were simple. When there was a slight pause in the conversation, or he was too drunk to talk, he'd dash towards the nearest open window and dive straight out, head first. His opponent, usually my good self, would attempt to prevent this by a pre-emptive rugby tackle to the waste or upper leg. If he was speedy enough, a desperate and frenzied final-second grasp for his ankles was deployed, to prevent Vom from exiting the room or moving vehicle via the window... simple.

He practiced frequently and became very good indeed, fast, supple and, most crucially, predictable. It was essential for at least one other participant to be playing, to understand the game-play, to recognise the body language and tell-tale eye movements in order to catch the flying drummer, lest he should break his ankle, leg or neck.

The first time that Mr Vom introduced me to 'out the window' was during the journey back from a concert. Spirits were high, and morale was good. We'd made our debut appearance a few days previously on 'Top Of The Pops' ('straight in at number 17'). The gig was full and fun, part of a successful run of tour dates. Vom and I sat in our usual back seat positions in a big blue bus and got cheerfully pissed. Wendi and Colette were sitting in the seats directly in front; talking Dexedrine-fuelled shit and listening to Hawkwind. Vom cunningly waited until the coach achieved top speed, manoeuvring across lanes and past high-sided lorries. Then in a flash and without warning, he slid open his window, clambered half out and politely knocked on Wendi's window; looking like a toy troll in a wind tunnel, scaring the shit out of her in the process. I clutched his belt and anchored him as best I could, my knuckles white and clenched. A 70mph wind blasted my face with motorway debris and beery saliva. He grinned inanely at the screaming backing singers, waving with friendly intent, tongue flapping with the smile of a travelling Labrador. He'd taken us all by surprise, shocked and entertained everyone and hadn't died; it was a solid start.

The power of 'out the window' could be used for the greater good as well as just for mischief and amusement. Some months later, on a Scandinavian tour, we were booked to play a Casino. We arrived the night before and checked into a hotel, The Stockholm Plaza, a modern many-storied hotel, with big shiny windows. As was often the case if we had a night off, we'd search for entertainment. However, we couldn't find anywhere open late enough and decided to hang out in our rooms, playing poker for bubblegum and drinking gin and orange. This was to be a mistake. We'd invited a young lighting guy along with us on tour, Whiz was his name, he promoted a psychedelic nightclub (The Taste Experience) and had oil-lamps and groovy light-wheels with which he illuminated our stages. He would later go on to be a successful film maker, but on this evening he chose to share secret gossip with me, McGuire and Mr Vom. Apparently, some bastard had been shagging McGuire's girlfriend. We were shocked, McGuire especially. The ambience suffered immediately; Whiz realised that he should have been less forthcoming. McGuire fell silent and sullen. I tried to keep chipper by downing several large neat gins at Mr Vom's insistence but to little effect; the relaxed, light-hearted atmosphere had vanished. Mr Vom took charge; all of a sudden he was up on his toes and sprinting towards the opened window at lightning speed. I watched through gin-glazed eyes as if viewing events in slow motion, reality too fast for my brain to comprehend. Whiz and McGuire sat mouth agog as Vom launched from the carpet, muscle memory streamlining his body into a perfect diving arc.

'Out the window,' he shouted as he flew through the air.

His cry momentarily cleared my head, these were his rules, and this was my cue. I threw myself at the window, the momentum of my shoulder deflecting his trajectory. My fingers just hooked his collar in time, my arms scraped and bloodied by the buckles of his winkle picker boots. He was safe. The moment of peril over, reeled in like a slippery fish, he collapsed into a chuckling heap at my feet, and I shut the window. Mr Vom had, in one swift danger defying movement, executed and survived another 'out the window' event and successfully changed the mood of the room for the better.

This was Mr Vom's greatest window experiment; events would never be quite as idyllic or ideal again. The Casino owner cancelled the show; not what he'd expected, and I was too hung over to sound-check.

McGuire began talking to himself, threatening unseen enemies with un-thrown fists and verbal fits of non-revenge. Whiz never toured with us again and became rich and famous.

Life went on regardless, but Mr Vom would eventually jump out a window to entertain a room full of partying people (who didn't know what he was doing), and he promptly broke his leg.

22. If

If I had a pound for every time that McGuire bought me a drink - I would have exactly one pound. I remember the occasion well; June 1986, it was an evening of great celebration. We were at Dingwalls in Camden Lock to see a band called Boys Wonder, a group for whom I had sometimes played and would at a later date join. Andy McNaughton, a gentleman who worked for IRS arrived at the bar, he was smiling. He had the midweek chart position for *Spirit In The Sky* and would share it with us if McGuire purchased us both a drink, which he did, begrudgingly. It was very good news.

We were to meet Mr Vom after the gig at Gossips; by the time we arrived I was really rather merry. I couldn't wait to tell Vom the news, but I insisted on another drink before I'd say anything else. Vom dutifully obliged with a pint of heavily watered Gossips lager in an ice-cold frosted glass.

'We are Number One,' I said.

Vom was dating an Italian stripper, the nicest of girls, with a younger sister who was even nicer, also a stripper. Blonde and beautiful with a double fit figure who, according to Mr Vom, had a crush on me. He was quite insistent on this fact. She was at Gossips also. Vom introduced us; we exchanged a few simple pleasantries before she leant in and kissed me, I kissed her in return and grabbed a handful of flesh and mini-skirt.

Almost immediately she recommended that we go back to her place. She lived in the same building as Vom's girlfriend, in rooms above The Intrepid Fox in Wardour St. I had heard stories of this place, stories of wonder and awe; three strippers in three rooms guarded by a fearsome kung-fu kicking landlord. The third stripper, the plainest of the three, was deep in conversation with McGuire, who would also later go back to this house of nudity and pleasure, as would Mr Vom.

We burst out into the warm evening air and ran down Meard Street hand in hand; a few seconds later we arrived, through the door, up the stairs, into her room and breathless. The nasty landlord was nowhere to be seen. She bolted the bedroom door securely behind, and we quickly undressed, hands rubbing and tongues knotted. The light from the street was all that lit her room; a constantly evolving palette of street lamps, flickering shop fronts, pub windows and the West End traffic. Its noise and chatter created the soundtrack to our excitement. We writhed and contorted, gasping for air as adrenalin raised our blood, eager, energetic and rude.

Some minutes later we were interrupted by calls coming up from the street, she rolled from the bed. Her sister, with the other stripper, Mr Vom and McGuire were outside, and they needed keys. I marvelled as she leaned through the window to throw a key fob. She was breathtaking, flawless. I jumped off the bed and pressed behind her; she giggled and pulled me back onto the mattress.

The house suddenly filled with noise, footsteps, bangs, cashes, shouting and laughter. The bedroom door rattled and shook in its frame as Mr Vom tested our defences

'Yeh, go on, Dickie Damage, wahaah, whaaaaaah... Dammmmaaage.'
The bolt held true as the racket dispersed into other rooms and other beds. We were left alone to resume our passions, saying nothing; desperate, intense, frenzied and animal.

We continued our exertions deep into the night; the air cooled, and eventually we did the same. As I sat back to rest, I realised that this was a life-defining moment. I was twenty-two years of age, the bass player for a successful rock and roll band; we were on 'Top of the Pops' and were Number One. To top everything, I was with this outrageously attractive and gloriously naked girl. It couldn't get any better than this.

I looked about the room properly for the first time; the forgiving neon glow was replaced by fresh dawn sunlight. She smiled and pointed to the wall next to her bed, a collage of pop star posters, record sleeves, music magazine articles and sellotape. She kissed the tip of her finger and touched one of the figures in a picture. I squinted at the wall to focus. It was a portrait photograph of me, carefully cut from the single sleeve. Next to this, from a poster, was another photo of me, the other band members missing, cut away and discarded. Next to this, from a magazine, a picture of me and another and another, the wall next to her bed was covered with pictures of me, just me. Some of which I didn't know existed.

'I love you,' she said.
Panic suddenly replaced reason; I could feel the hair on my arm standing on end and my hands shaking. This was no college-girl crush, or super groupie one-nighter, this was proper grown-up trouble, a stalker, an obsession, with repercussions.

'I have a girlfriend,' I said nervously.
She covered her mouth and trembled. Her eyes filled with water, and my thoughts turned to the scary landlord, a man that famously attacked strangers in his house where boys were banned.

'For how long?' She sobbed.
I really did have a girlfriend (Mads) who would have murdered me if she had found out.

'We are engaged,' I lied, unconvincingly.
I needed to get out of the building. An upset stripper mixed with an over-protective martial-artist minder spelt imminent danger to any musician.

'Sorry,' I told her, 'I have to leave now.'
I dressed quickly; she pulled on a t-shirt, unbolted her door and led me through the sleeping house. Vom was out cold, I noticed a crumpled pile of grey underwear and snoring sheets that I recognised as McGuire.
She unlocked the front door and stood in the doorway; I felt her gaze follow as I crossed the road and walked off into the new morning.

It was a great night, I loved it, crazy and mad, and so was she. Beautiful and furious, her name was Laura, and she never spoke to me again.

Mr Vom was later to confide that as he left the house later that day, the pavement beneath her bedroom window was scattered with the scraps of discarded record sleeves, defaced photographs and torn up posters, all of me.

23. One

We were performing *Spirit In The Sky* nightly whilst
on tour with The Damned and American freak-beat
band The Fuzztones; it went down surprisingly well,
the crowd dutifully bought the record the following
day, but they weren't the only ones. Thanks to our
involvement with Alice In Wonderland and thorough
gigging, we had built a solid and varied fan base.
Punks liked us due to our connection with The
Damned and other support slots with the old-school
punk glitterati, The Revillos, Chelsea and Spear Of
Destiny. Hippies knew us through slots with
Hawkwind, The Pink Fairies and Ozric Tentacles.
Mods saw us play with garage greats The Prisoners,
right-on stompers The Red Skins and energetic mod-
niks The Playn Jayn. Goths knew us from concerts
with Killing Joke, New Model Army, Flesh For Lulu,
The Cardiacs and The Cult (The Anadin Brothers
made a cameo appearance in The Cult's video - *Rain*).
Psychobillies loved us; we played with The Meteors,
The Milkshakes and The Stingrays. We even picked up
a small psychobilly fan club, who called themselves
The Custard Beasts (led by a large-nosed youth named
Bogie). These flat-headed slam-dancers instigated
activity in our mosh-pit, a heaving broth of thrashing
forearms, bruising shoulders and jabbing elbows - not
for the faint-hearted. So, along with the flower-
children that frequented Gossips, we had great and
loyal fans.

It was these fans who first bought the single, breaking it into the UK Charts, putting our pointy boot through the door. The radio play generated a whole new audience, one that had never heard of Doctor and the Medics but enjoyed the single, which they subsequently purchased. Then, once we were on 'Top Of The Pops', we gained the attention of the masses, kids with pocket money and paper round wages, mums, dads and grandparents who bought a record every now and then - an opportunity to use an otherwise redundant record token. Disc Jockeys bought it to play in discos, pubs and clubs. Amateur DJs bought it to play at school discos, weddings and garden fêtes. Our friends bought it, our families bought it, and our teachers bought it. People who didn't even like it bought it. The whole country bought it. Before we knew it we were Number One and dressed to thrill. Frills, sparkles and glitter, satin capes and flares with sheer silk shirts open to the hip; reinventing 70s glam rock for the 80s kids. I thought that I looked like a chocolate box and tied a red ribbon around my purple bass to complete the confectionery ensemble. We donned white outfits to match our 'spirit' guide. Our fifteen minutes of fame... ready, steady. Go!

A lackey from MCA took us out after our No.1 appearance on TOTP, for another slap-up curry. We were used to these heady restaurant excesses by now, we knew how to work it and over-ate and over-drank until we were barely conscious. It was a moment to savour; everything was going to be different from now on. I pinched my arm to see if this was real. We were pop stars now, like the pop stars that we'd watched growing up as wide-eyed children. Like Bolan, Bowie and Black Sabbath. The bands we watched as kids, Slade, The Sweet and T-Rex. Like the music heroes who wrote the rules, The Stones, Cream and The Who; fast girls, sports cars, big houses with swimming pools and parties every night, this would surely become our new lifestyle. We were going to be rich and famous, I would live in a castle, marry a fashion model and drive an E-Type Jag; it would be everything that we'd ever dreamed of.

Later that night at the bar in Gossips someone asked me quietly:

'Are you a millionaire now?'

I didn't reply, but I, like everyone else, naively assumed that Number One = Millionaire.

24. Scala

The second time that I fell over on stage was during a performance at the Scala Cinema, during one of several Alice In Wonderland Psychedelic Film Festival all-nighters. As the name suggests, a handful of cult sixties movies were shown throughout the night with a live band intermission. 'Blow Up', 'Psych Out', 'Stones in the Park' and 'Performance', the usual film favourites amongst 60s fans, with the occasional special feature. Sometimes there would be sixties television commercials or documentaries about fashion, David Bailey, Mary Quant or Biba. On at least two occasions a unique independent British film was shown entitled *I Keep Thinking It's Tuesday* starring Richard Searle the Psychedelic Beatnik. This was supposed to be a short film to promote the club Alice In Wonderland, shot in Greenwich Park and Gossips; featuring various club regulars, some of The Medics and Roman Jug. However, when Clive and Christian Paris watched the footage they decided that it looked shit, so they edited themselves out, my bits remained. I wasn't at the edit.

On the night of my second stage fall, during the live Medics set, Clive shoved me across the stage 'for effect'; I stumbled and tripped over backwards, collapsing against my amplifier, which in turn fell against the cinema screen. My pink paisley trousers were too tight for me to stand up, so I plonked away in a helpless heap until help arrived; a roadie had to hoist me to my feet whilst I played. Fortunately, the screen wasn't damaged.

The audience were mostly frazzled on something or another. As well as alcohol, lots of hallucinogens and amphetamines were imbibed, to help stay the course of the long hours. Multiple seats of speeding freakniks packed into restricting rows, uncomfortable and claustrophobic, legs cramped, eyes sore, slumped and fidgety; planning their chances of escape to the toilet; eventually becoming sick of sitting in a stuffy cinema with five hundred stinking hippies, or urine soaked homeless types that snuck in without paying to sleep in the celluloid flickering warmth.

One such whiffy street dweller caused a stir when he avoided the bored security staff, negotiated the darkened stairs and entered the heart of the cinema midway through the night. As punters watched the disturbing footage of The Rolling Stones struggling with the dregs of flower power in *Gimme Shelter*, the homeless man found the gentlemen's toilet on the top floor, opened the window and jumped out. Speeding punks and hallucinating hippies narrowly avoided a bad trip en masse, as Metropolitan policemen arrived to investigate the suicide of an unknown individual. They were fairly discreet, but it spooked Christian Paris, who, as the individual in charge, had to deal with the matter, desperately trying to appear 'normal' while sporting love beads, bleached hair and smudged mascara.

25. Tube

We had some good bands support us over the years,
The Twenty Flight Rockers (Newcastle Riverside),
The Stone Roses (The Croydon Underground, July 4th
1985), Gaye Bykers on Acid (The Town & Country,
Kentish Town), The Shamen (also at The
Underground) and The Queerboys (Greenwich Tunnel
Club), to name just five. A good support band keeps
you on your toes, no room for complacency; you have
to work hard for your audience. Being blown off stage
by your support act is never good. We supported
Pleasure and The Beast (a theatrical horror outfit) at
The Clarendon Hammersmith and blew them off stage,
they were furious. When they were booked to support
us in return, at Crocs in Essex, they worked twice as
hard and blew us away.

Zodiac Mindwarp and the Love Reaction
were particularly good; they supported us often, and
were always excellent. Also Alice in Wonderland
regulars, they had a high profile with record labels
sniffing and were accordingly invited to appear on
Channel 4's ground-breaking music television show
'The Tube', when we were asked to close the show.
They were good - but that night we were better.

Everyone watched 'The Tube'; it was part of
the Friday night ritual. We were invited to headline a
special one-off edition, broadcast live for the first time
throughout Europe, called 'The Euro-Tube'. Filmed in
a dedicated television studio in Newcastle, we drove
up the night before and tried to take it easy in the hotel

bar. We didn't want to risk a ruinous hangover; the programme would have a massive television audience, so we went to bed at a reasonable hour, sober. Nothing was left to chance, even the roadies stayed sober. Next morning, however, we were rudely woken by Martin Pyle.

'Bad news,' he said, 'the van's been stolen.' The Medics mobile, a converted transit van, contained, as well as all of The Anadin Brothers' stage clothes (and a bag of fresh carrots), our musical equipment. Drums, sticks, guitars, basses, strings, picks, cables, leads, plugs, flight cases and amplifiers, everything essential for a band to play live.

'Get up,' Martin said, 'we have to buy new gear.'
The theft was covered by our insurance policy, so we rushed into the biggest music store that we could find to replace everything that the thieving scum-bags had stolen. Drums, sticks, guitars, basses, strings, picks, cables, leads, plugs, flight cases and amplifiers; the shop keeper was delighted

Meanwhile, Wendi and Colette went shopping amongst Newcastle's premier head shops and charity Boutiques for replacement clothes. Clive appeared on local radio appealing for The Anadin Brothers' stage costumes to be returned; they apparently 'could never be replaced.'

As luck would have it, an hour before sound-check, the radio station received a call. The van had been found. Unable to break the huge padlock on the rear doors and having no use for the assortment of garish women's psychedelic dresses, the thieves abandoned the vehicle empty-handed, save for the bag of carrots that they took for their trouble. The brand new musical back-line was returned to the music store, the money refunded. The shop keeper was distraught.

The broadcast was very successful, one of our better TV performances to date, this despite syrup-wearing kiddie-fiddler Gary Glitter invading the stage during our final song. Clive was nearly upstaged by the since shamed paedophile's famous glam posturing, but he kept a tight grip on his microphone, and Glitter didn't manage to steal the show.

Back at the hotel we set about to destroy our livers as best we could to make up for the sobriety of the previous evening; we wanted to celebrate. Clive challenged me to a beer drinking race. This is something at which I'd won money before, and he was determined to win his money back. The rules were simple; I had to drink a freshly poured can of Newcastle Brown ale, from a straight pint glass, quicker than Clive could. However, there was no limit, and Clive could determine when to stop. His intention being that I would get so drunk that he would eventually drink a pint faster than me; one pint was all he needed to win the competition. Clive was a notorious cheat, but there were only four cans on the table, so I agreed to these terms. We shook hands, and then Clive produced a crate of twenty-four tins of Newcastle Brown from the back of the van

I bettered Clive for about six pints, I could gulp down the sweet beer in two or three big swigs, but it really hurt. My stomach would swell instantly with beer and gas, requiring repeated burping to remove the air from my painfully swollen gut. Clive just drank his pint steadily, not too fast; he'd planned for quantity and insisted on pouring another and another. After a couple of pints I'd have to rush off to the toilets for a much needed piss, my bladder bursting; the sprint to the Gents becoming faster each trip. Every time that I dashed to the toilet, there would be another pint freshly poured by Clive, happily sitting with a big grin on his face; the smug smirk of a man who was pouring brandy into my beer. Every pint that he'd poured was spiked with a rhinoceros-sedating measure of cheap Cognac. I became very quickly, paralytic. He won his money back off of me after about sixty minutes and I staggered off to find my hotel room, bouncing from wall to wall.

I was sharing a room with McGuire; he'd disappeared early with an implausibly attractive local named Justine; he'd had enough time to finish his dirty work, and I needed to crash so headed for bed. The room was up in the higher levels, I negotiated the lift successfully, but once in the corridor I couldn't remember the room number. I pushed the lift call button and boarded the lift to return to the lobby, but I fell out onto another floor as the doors dinged open. I was lost, and, what was worse, I urgently needed to shit. I desperately ran down the corridors looking for a toilet, nothing. I opened a fire-door and clambered up some stairs out onto yet another floor, my buttocks clenched, again nothing. I managed to call another lift; it went down but again opened to yet another toilet free floor. Squeezing my cheeks and waddling like a Mallard duck, I darted down an unlit corridor; I had no choice, I was going to have to find a quiet place. I'd defecate in a fire-escape stairwell. I crouched in a darkened alcove at the end of the corridor and took a large relieving dump.

I wandered back up the corridor as a door suddenly opened; it was McGuire, letting Justine out. I fell inside, collapsed on my bed and sank into a heavy drunken sleep until the following morning.

Bags packed, shaved and showered, we checked out of the hotel room. I had a vague memory of my toilet indiscretion the night before and decided to return to the scene of the crime. I retraced my steps down the hallway to view the incriminating evidence, the stool in a fire-escape; but as hard as I searched I couldn't find it, there was nothing. Not only was there no trace of my evacuation, there was, more confusingly, no fire escape. At the end of the corridor was a small dark alcove but with a hotel room tucked away into its recess. I strained my memory, trying to determine if I'd imagined the whole thing, a bad dream maybe. Or if an unfortunate cleaner had already removed the offending item - and in my drunken stupor I'd simply shat outside someone's door.

26. Gobbing

No one ever spat at us until Mr Vom joined the band.
His arrival not only heralded a new era in which I
would find myself avoiding his saliva during
rehearsals (Vom spat when drunk), but the nature of
the shows themselves, especially if Roman joined us
on stage, involved lots and lots of gobbing. The
Damned audience were of a spitting kind, and this
rubbed off on us. Mr Vom sometimes enjoyed spitting
back at the audience which only served to encourage
them. Fortunately, this phase passed once we appeared
on 'Top Of The Pops', but until that moment the
gobbing fraternity made their presence felt.

During these early, pre-chart hit shows (the ones that
appealed to punks, with Roman on guitar) we tailored
our stage clothes to suit, lots of black materials,
studded belts, no garish colours. But this had a serious
disadvantage, one which we discovered at our peril
whilst on a short run of gigs 'up North'; we played a
concert at Scunthorpe Baths. Clive wore black leather
trousers, a black satin shirt with a matching black
velvet cape. As he walked out onto the stage, an
audience of Scunthorpe's finest greeted him with a
torrent of projectile spittle; the stage lights dimmed,
blocked out by a blanket of thick phlegm that rained
down like archers arrows, a hail storm of green grolly;
Clive was covered head to foot in the disgusting slime.
His clothes dripping and hair clotted. His face
glistened with coughed-up mucus. The rest of us tried

our best to move to the back of the stage, to keep a low profile, but Clive had no choice, his black clothes were completely soiled, smeared with filthy whites, greys and yellows as he darted between the PA speakers, long stalactites of wet sputum hanging from his microphone hand as he sang. Back in the dressing room he peeled off his clothes, dropped them into a dustbin liner and hosed himself down. We never wore black for punk audiences ever again; black is a target.

A punk with a nasty cold is never a welcome sight in a mosh-pit, hoiking up lumps of bacterial matter, rolling it into balls around his tongue and squinting as he takes careful aim. Roman told us that The Damned's audiences took to half sucking the chocolate covered honeycomb sweets Maltesers, then spitting them at the band; they were easier to aim than phlegm, plus a mouthful could be sprayed over a wider area.

There was an urban legend amongst bands that you could catch hepatitis from other people's saliva; rumours circulated about various drummers falling victim to this (they can't dodge the gobbing). The drummer from UK Subs was one, the drummer from The Rezillos also. We'd heard of this rumour when we were asked to support the Revillos (The Rezillos changed their name) at Portsmouth University. We went down well, The Revillos, however, did not. We watched in amazement as their glamorous female vocalist Fay Fife stormed off stage after being repeatedly spat at by skinheads, disappointed by the band's new, less punky direction. This, after hammering the gobbing louts with her microphone and stamping on their shaved heads with the spiked heel of her stiletto thigh boots.

As The Revillos left the stage we exited by the fire escape and ran for the safety of the van. The skinheads were getting nasty, fights were already breaking out.

Clive stopped us in our tracks, 'listen,' he said, pointing back to the venue.

The audience was an angry mob, and the angry mob was chanting:

> 'Medics!
> Medics!
> Medics!'

27. London

Eagle-eyed viewers, those who bothered to watch until
the very end of the final credits, will have seen a few
frames of one of the oddest images to ever air on 'The
Tube' or any other music television programme. The
closing seconds of the 'Euro-Tube' featured the Doctor
and the Medics' famous exploding Vicar's Head. This
fraction of a second flash of explosives, smoke, papier-
mâché and chicken wire was in fact a replica
Exploding Vicar's Head, the original having been
successfully detonated during one of our London
shows a few weeks earlier.

We always tried to do something special for
London gigs, to go that little bit extra. At our first
headline slot at The Hammersmith Palais we had
twenty Anadin Brothers on stage, bunched behind and
between the back-line. For another show, at the
Kentish Town Town & Country Club, we erected a
giant wooden skateboard half-pipe complete with pro-
American skateboarders, the band equipment was set
up in the middle of the ramp. But arguably our most
ambitious London gig, again at the T&C, featured
Doctor and the Medics as headline act, with support
from Doctor and the Medics and an opening slot by
Doctor and the Medics. We were to play three times.
This concert, as I made my entrance front of house,
was the third time that I fell over on stage, slipping on
a film of oily water that a lighting man sprayed into
the air to better illuminate his laser show. The opening
act, us but without the girls, comprised of our very

110

first attempts at songwriting, *Secrets Of A Baby's Mind, Damaged Brains, Dalek In The Toilet* and *Pink People*; fast, furious, and refreshing for us to play again.

The second act, us again, was one long version of the garage classic *Gloria*, starting again just with the bare bones of The Medics, joined by the girls then followed by a succession of 'celebrity' musicians. Lemmy, from Motörhead, who played my spare bass. From The Damned was Dave Vanian on extra vocals and Rat Scabies on an extended drum kit set around Mr Vom. Various members of the Hendrix-obsessed band Voodoo Child shared extra guitar duties, as did Roman Jug. There was a slight altercation between Scabies and Mr Vom during the song crescendo, but it quickly fizzled away. The whole glorious jam was only supposed to run for 10 minutes but easily ran for over twice that amount of time; the audience were very patient, very drunk or both.

The headline set was in fact two sets, by us yet again. Clive and the girls left the stage for a full costume change halfway through, the rest of us filled in with a couple of instrumentals to plug the gap, Clive reappeared ahead of the girls, for two or three more numbers, before the Anadin Brothers made a second entrance. It was a long night, The Medics, The Medics and nothing but The Medics.

The Exploding Vicar's Head featured at the skateboard ramp concert. In the run of interviews leading up to the gig Clive plugged the show as best he could; on one occasion he boasted (in an off the cuff outburst of surrealist humour and without considering the practicalities) that, as well as a spectacular line-up of bands, there would be an exploding vicar's head. This announcement caused some confusion as well as great excitement. So much so that Christian Paris dutifully constructed a life-size, lifelike sculpture that resembled the great British actor David Niven, resplendent with his tidy moustache, receding hair, spectacles and, of course, a vicar's dog collar. It looked very dignified and was proudly displayed throughout our set. Clive pretended to communicate with it between songs as it nestled next to the drums, chatting as if it was real. On the closing chord of our final encore, a massive charge of gun powder, carefully packed within the realistically painted head, was ignited. Very few people got the joke; we left the stage to wild applause and screams of horror mixed. Some people thought that they'd witnessed a tragic accident; for those intrepid souls, tripping on mushrooms or LSD, the Exploding Vicar's Head looked like an elderly version of Clive - they thought we'd just detonated his father.

28. Fame

During the opening number of our debut appearance at The Marquee Club in Wardour Street, supporting '77 punks', Chelsea, long before we signed a record deal, fuelled with adrenalin and the innocent enthusiasm of a man willing to do anything to help the progression of our cause, Clive leapt from the stage in a half-executed backward somersault into the crowd. He cracked his head on the edge of the stage and fell unconscious on the floor. He was carried to the dressing room behind the stage by Gene October (Chelsea's singer) whilst we improvised a lengthy middle-eight instrumental section and Wendi finished Clive's vocal parts; we prepared to leave the stage after one song, and take him straight to hospital. However, as we struck the final chord, the dressing room door burst open, and Clive re-appeared counting us into our second number. He sat on the drum riser and finished the set. My eyes glossed with admiration at this selfless commitment to our shared purpose and to his friends.

Fame changes everything, and when Clive experienced it, he changed dramatically and not for the better. The moment of his metamorphosis from our funny, loyal friend into the opposite can be pin-pointed to a singular moment in time; the day after our second TOTP appearance ('zooming up the charts at Number 3'), on the phone in Andrew King's office, during a light-hearted interview with Radio One DJ Bruno Brookes.

Bruno was a fan of the band; he loved the single and played tracks from the album. He scheduled a pre-recorded interview with Clive to be aired during his popular tea-time programme, funny and radio friendly, an insight into the crazy world of the wacky Doctor. I sat in silence with Andrew and McGuire as Clive began his interview, smiling at his witticisms, the well-used one-liners that usually amused. McGuire was the first to stop smiling; Clive was asked to give a brief description of each band member in the form of an answer to a humorous question.

'Why wouldn't I like to sit next to them in a restaurant?' Bruno joked.
This sounded like it was going to be fun. Andrew pretended to clap his hands in anticipation, McGuire gave me a wink, we were going to enjoy this - but we didn't. Cruel would be the best way to describe Clive's remarks.

'McGuire is so obese and smells so bad that nobody wants to sit next to him in a restaurant.'
Andrew forced a smile in our direction, but the jibe wasn't funny, just needlessly hurtful. It was then my turn to be bad-mouthed.

'Richard is so dull and miserable that nobody wants to....'
He continued to describe the band with vicious snipes, which I didn't recognise, neither did my friends or parents when they listened to the broadcast, they too were upset by Clive's 'humour'.

From that moment onwards Clive became very sarcastic, boorish and a generally unpleasant person to be around. He would laugh at anyone's misfortune. Any occasion to be obnoxious was utilised and relished. In an interview in the pop magazine *Smash*

Hits, in which he was asked to list his least favourite things, I was on the list. My friend worked for *Smash Hits*, she called me and offered to remove my name from the article; she thought it mean, but I pretended to be unmoved, and it was published. The practical jokes seemed spiteful; a friendly game could be turned into an ordeal. He took advantage of his height; he bruised my cheek during a pillow fight. I swung a large foam cushion; Clive slipped a fist inside his cushion cover and punched me square in the face. Clive could be a bully, he broke Mr Vom's nose.

The ego was out of hand. Christian noticed as well, when discussing a forthcoming London show, Christian jokingly suggested that, whilst on stage...

'The Doctor should announce that he is the new Messiah.'

Clive imagined that he was an artist of importance, a pop legend with a persona to suit, another Alice Cooper or Ziggy Stardust. Photo sessions evolved into personality performances. He flexed his muscles for the shots, clenching his fists, breathing heavily and tensing the veins in his neck; energy and intensity personified for the camera, the living embodiment of a rock'n'roll god. The rest of us ignored him, it was embarrassing.

In a hotel bar on one occasion Clive mortified us by challenging Siouxsie and The Banshees to a football match. They sat quietly chatting amongst themselves; Clive barged into their conversation, uninvited.

'We'll play you at football, and we'll beat you,' he slurred aggressively.

'We don't play with wankers,' The Banshees replied.

With any addiction, be it to drugs, sex, alcohol or fame, the first step to recovery is to admit that you have a problem; in a succession of brief but sincere exchanges with band individuals and selected crew, Clive apologised for his behaviour during this intoxicating period of fame. Some time later, at The Marquee 2 in Charing Cross Rd, he shook my hand and told me that, I …

'… was an excellent bassist.'

I recognised this to be Clive's apology to me, and I accepted it in good faith. He smiled warmly and held my gaze until sure that I understood the gravitas of his words; and I returned the compliment.

'You are an excellent front-man.' I said.

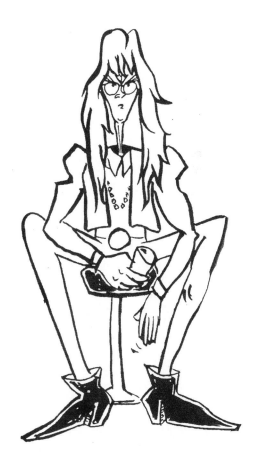

29. Scum

The fourth time that I fell over on stage was during the final song of our headline show at the London Hammersmith Palais. I attempted to execute a running judo roll across the stage, a move that I'd seen the legendary John Otway perform on several occasions. I mistimed and misjudged the exercise, collapsing onto my knees and in a crumpled heap at the feet of twenty assorted men and women dressed as Anadin Brothers. I brazened the fall, Medics audiences were used to witnessing such stumbles, and there was always the possibility that nobody had noticed.

The first time that Clive fell over on stage everyone noticed, it was at The Riley Smith Hall in Leeds. As always he'd march onto the stage a short way through an instrumental introduction, his cape held open like velvet wings, strutting like a Gothic peacock. The audience always cheered.

'Alright Leeds?' he bellowed with a deliberate American drawl; unfortunately he then wedged his pointed shoe between two monitor speakers, span around in a half pirouette and fell backward in an awkward cacophony of bangs, thumps and groans. Unable to untangle himself from his cape, microphone cable and heavy speakers, he thrust his microphone aloft like Excalibur from a misty lake, the audience were just able to glimpse his raised fist and hear the giggles of embarrassment punctuating the music. The rest of us finished the opening song without vocals.

After the gig, a peculiar gentleman strolled backstage to introduce himself; he was the first of two people who we were to befriend, happy to call themselves Scum. The second Scum, Uncle Scum, was a roadie for Alice In Wonderland favourites, Voodoo Child. A small bearded, denim-clad biker that smelt of motor oil and cigarettes. Voodoo Child often supported us, and he'd tried to give his band an edge by getting me fuck-faced before stage time.

'Smoke this little number, it'll loosen you up,' he'd insist, 'you can trust your Uncle Scum.'
I blatantly couldn't trust Uncle Scum, but he was a nice enough bloke and made me laugh. And stoned.

The first Scum, the one that wandered into our dressing room in Leeds, explained that we should call him Scum (legally his middle name) even though his first name was Dave. His full name, which he'd officially registered by Deed Poll, was Mr Dave Scum Vanian. He liked The Damned.

Dave Scum Vanian had many tattoos. If you were in a punk band then you featured somewhere on the inky skin of Dave Scum Vanian. He told us that he enjoyed our gig, especially the bit when Clive...

'... fell on his feckin' arse,' and agreed to treat himself to another tattoo, a Doctor and the Medics tattoo. We were his newest favourite punk band.

We received a letter from Scum some months later, with an enclosed photograph of his latest tattoo, but our paths were not destined to cross again for a year or so, when we were Number One in the pop charts.

'Fecking, sell-out pop band, Doctor and the fecking Medics, cunts,' he said as he opened his shirt to reveal his dirty green Doctor and the Medics tattoo.

30. Burn

The debut album, *Laughing At The Pieces*, contained
some of the highlights of our set; *Love Peace And
Bananas, Fried Egg Bad Monday* and *The Smallness
Of The Mustard Pot*, but the recording sounded tiny in
comparison to how we played live. The long hours
trying to get the drums to sound like Jon Bonham, the
guitar like Angus Young or the bass like John
Entwistle were wasted; when the album was mixed it
was, for us and our hard-core fans, a limp
disappointment. Released a few weeks after our chart
success, it did moderately well (a UK Chart position of
twenty-five), but it wasn't long before it appeared in
the cheap buckets and clearance bins of Woolworth
and Tesco.

We hated the sleeve; a photo of Clive looking
guilty, like he'd just been caught masturbating, framed
by small boxes containing band shots. The typography
utilised a 'pagan' Celtic font (Wendi's idea) that jarred
with the kitsch photography and some backwards
lyrics (mirror writing). The final thing looked more
like a Christmas advent calendar than an album cover.
We offered to replace the sleeve with hand-drawn
alternatives if people sent us their original, which took
us months. I felt sorry for the fans who received some
of these hastily scribbled felt-tip pen 'collectables', a
few were quite good but McGuire's especially were
truly shit.

IRS called a meeting to discuss a follow-up
single; company man Andy McNaughton suggested

No One Loves You When You've Got No Shoes, a big groovy riff number influenced by Blood Sweat And Tears, very popular live, with lyrics about Rasputin the mad barefooted Russian monk. Unfortunately his suggestion was ignored, A&R man Steve Tannett sent us back to Craig Leon's apartment for a brain-storming second-hit-single writing session.

After several hours of playing Cream riffs backwards, and Clive knotting his brow whilst crooning flowery sentences about cow pastures and hemlock, we gave up. The record label called urgent discussions with the management to brood over the possibility of another cover version; we were not invited - so we took it upon ourselves to do what we did best, play. We booked a full band rehearsal and knocked up a new tune, a heavy soul number called *Burn*.

Burn was again influenced by funky stuff, Hendrix meets Sly And The Family Stone; we quickly recorded a demo, and it was cool. IRS were on board; it would be the follow-up to *Spirit In The Sky*. Craig Leon was to produce, again at Britannia Row with the same engineer, Graham Meek; it took a day. The finished track, again, had all of the guts and gusto methodically removed and sounded nothing like the demo, but at least it was our song, we'd written it. Craig told us that it was good and sounded like another hit. And again we chose to believe him.

We also chose to assume that *Burn* would go straight to number one, and that we'd be back on 'Top Of The Pops' to perform it. There were pre-emptive discussions over whether we should play *Burn* on the Christmas TOTP Special rather than *Spirit In The Sky*; we'd rather mime to our own song than a cover version. We included the new 'future chart hit' in our live set, with a much heavier feel naturally, and it went down a treat. A new photo session was booked for the single sleeve and another video scheduled with the same team and director that made the previous one.

Burn was gonna be hot.

31. Mystery

One of Christian Paris's better ideas was the Alice In
Wonderland Magical Mystery Trip. Hundreds of
ticket-holding funny-haired freakniks were coached,
trained and herded by a 'pied-piper' from pre-arranged
meeting points in London to secret locations
throughout England for a big bastard party. There were
four Mystery Trips sited in exciting mind-expanding
venues; Chislehurst Caves (ancient hand-carved
caverns quarried from the living rock by druids),
Butlins Holiday camp (a nostalgic playground of
kitsch and glitter in the once thriving Essex holiday
destination of Clacton), an antiquated wooden pier in
the sleepy Norfolk seafaring town of Lowestoft - and a
warehouse in Battersea.

In October 1984, the first event flyer
advertised 'a sensational place somewhere in England,
a place you have never been to before, nor are likely to
go again'. It turned out to be Chislehurst Caves, much
to the disappointment of south London locals, who still
had to travel from the meeting point in Hyde Park to a
venue they knew well, and where parties and club
nights were frequently held. However, decorated with
the trademark Alice toilet roll and psychedelic light
show, it was a party like they'd never before
experienced. The six hundred attendees were ushered
in through the narrow caves by a large brown bear
wearing Converse All Stars, where the majority of
them dropped hallucinogens or bought raffle tickets to
win beer from the bar. Various circus curiosities and

psychedelic entertainments added to the otherworldly atmosphere. The dirt floor was soft and uneven, sodden with beer and hippie sweat that made people totter around as if at sea. Despite the police banging on the large bolted iron doors (an unsuccessful to attempt to raid the event) and a power cut that created total pitch-black, everyone remained relaxed and panic free. The sight of a man in a grizzly bear costume dragging an industrial power cable through the crowd with a torch between his teeth, oddly put would-be Acid casualties at ease, and both power and equilibrium was quickly restored.

The Medics' set was a highlight of the night. During an impromptu performance of Led Zeppelin's *Whole Lotta Love* (featuring Roman Jug on second guitar) I noticed a familiar face in the crowd. Sweating at the front of the stage was a kid who I recognised from school. David George (a hardcore soapy-haired punk rocker who was in my sixth form Maths group) was staring wide-eyed and smiling, his dilated pupils and cud-chewing jaw betraying the Acid in his blood. He never acknowledged me at school; I was a mod and Jam fan. His favourite band were worthy anarchic do-gooders Crass, and here he was punching the moist air along to our trash thrash. I swallowed back a tear of pride, a salty, perspiration soaked tear that stung my eyes and made me squint - but a tear nevertheless.

The second Magical Mystery Trip was greatly anticipated due to the success of the first but was organised hastily and rushed through a couple of months later. Billed as 'a place where wizards have their wands recharged, where goblins sit on mushrooms and count the stars'; it turned out to be the disused and dilapidated Decca Records warehouse in an industrial estate, with a voucher system bar selling Carlsberg Special Brew. Despite the oil-lamp drenched drapery, a full-on laser show, a mood-altering synthesiser sound-scape and day-glow minstrels serenading by a bubbling fake waterfall, it was still just a gig in a big square room. The Medics played again but this time supported by 'an authentic sixties garage band' called The Cockroaches. Word quickly spread that this mysterious band of wizened longhairs was a secret gig by Naz Nomad and The Nightmares, a side project of The Damned. But it was, in fact, Alex Bienkov (our occasional tour manager) plus a couple of members from the band that became Boys Wonder and me wearing my mother's wig. As the sun rose, and we evacuated the venue, we noticed Christian Paris, sobbing. He'd purchased a thousand cans of out of date Special Brew, expecting to sell the lot at a healthy profit. Unless you live in a cardboard box, you would be hard pushed to drink more than a couple of tins of Special Brew. Hippies on LSD, especially, don't drink high strength lager. He sold virtually nothing and lost a small fortune.

The third Mystery Trip, summer of '85, 'a cosmic ballroom very rarely visited', was Butlins in Clacton. Christian needed to make up for the preceding warehouse party and planned Butlins well. Loaded into trains at Liverpool Street Station and then decanted into coaches, excited punters finally found themselves at the holiday resort, welcomed by fire jugglers and giant-headed stilt walkers. As well as the usual fun attractions (the Alice In Wonderland psychedelic disco and light-show, circus acts and atmosphere enhancing decorations), the all-nighter had extra attractions, an alien monster cabaret, a sixties

film show and lots and lots of bands. Ring Of Roses,
The Magic Mushroom Band, The Treatment, The
Volcanoes, Perfect Disaster, The Surfin' Lungs,
Another Green World and Bad Acid & The Spooks,
the latter being another secret Medics line-up. It was
the best Mystery Trip and a total success that went
without hitch - apart from Clive cutting open his
forearm on a protruding nail as he climbed a post on
stage during the secret line-up spot. He ran off stage,
jumped in a car bound for the nearest hospital for
stitches and a bandage and then back to Butlins ready
for the headline act, Doctor and the Medics.

As myth and legend began to surround the Mystery
Trips, the events sold out within days of the tickets
going on sale. Nothing like these had happened since
the Acid Trip Festivals and Freak Outs of the sixties,
there was pressure to impress. The fourth and final
event was held eleven months later on June 27th 1986.
Spirit In The Sky was in the pop charts and kebab-shop
boy band Wham played their farewell concert at
Wembley. Christian pulled out all the stops and hired a
Victorian seaside pier. Again a bevy of great support
bands filled the bill including Zodiac Mindwarp and
the Love Reaction, Voodoo Child, Mournblade, plus
several chaotic, spontaneous and depraved
entertainments; the crucifixion of cherished childhood
toys, naked ballroom dancing and a mock-Roman
orgy. But this trip was tormented by logistical
nightmares. Lucky ticket holders were to rendezvous
at Speakers Corner in Hyde Park to be driven by a
fleet of coaches; however, many vehicles arrived very
late, the coach drivers got lost and were simply scared
of their passengers. Many coaches didn't arrive for the
return trip. The drivers refused to drive freaks,

weirdoes and 'druggies' or just couldn't be bothered. Hundreds of exhausted and fucked-up flower children were strewn across Lowestoft beach, smelly and incoherent, whilst an overly pale Christian Paris frantically arranged alternative transport to take everyone home.

Mr Vom noticed McGuire's hairy white arse, wobbling up and down in the unforgiving morning sunlight as he surreptitiously shagged his girlfriend. Her transport still to arrive and with ankles around her shoulders, a small crowd gathered to watch; something to do, anything to help fill the long and arduous hours wait for the...

'... fucking coaches to arrive.'

32. Holland

As hundreds of exhausted Magical Mystery Trippers waited on Lowestoft beach, make-up smudged, tummies rumbling and chins hardened with crystalline saliva, we witnessed a handful of coaches finally arriving to return the unhappy trippers on their long journey home to bed. The Medics, on the other hand, just needed to drive a few miles down the road to Harwich harbour; we'd reserved some bunk beds in cabins, on a ferry bound for sunny Holland.

Rested up and settled into our comfortable Dutch beach-side hotel, we checked out the local sites. We were playing at an open-air festival the following evening with Californian flibbertigibbets The Bangles and Camden nutty boys Madness. The Bangles were heavily guarded by their boyfriends, so once we'd all had an ogle at Susanna Hoffs, we headed for a club. The keyboard player from Madness, a local session player from Greenwich named Shamus, was in the club; happy to chat to other Englishmen, we shared a few icy beers before hitting the hay. The gig had a late start the following evening; we had all day to ourselves, so decided to get up at a reasonable hour and hit the beach.

The weather was great; Mr Vom and I found a spot on the clean sand, quickly followed by McGuire and Martin Pyle. Neither Clive nor Wendi had beach-friendly attire so Wendi dragged Colette around some beachwear shops for company, whilst Clive eventually joined us wearing some candy-striped hipster trousers and carrying a large, colourful hired beach umbrella. The beach was quite busy; groups of bronzed Dutchmen and perfect Dutch girls lazed around on towels, recliners and deck chairs. The view was very nice; it was a topless beach.

We stayed for a couple of hours, Colette eventually managed to join us, but we were quite glad when it was time to leave. Whilst the rest of us enjoyed the sea and the sun, snoozing and chilling, trying not to letch at the ladies, Clive sat underneath his circus clown umbrella in his matching trousers, squinting at the Dutch tits.

'Stop staring,' the girls shouted, the boyfriends flexing muscles threateningly in readiness to thump the English beach pervert.
We were embarrassed, so Clive stared even more and made binocular shapes with his hands.

The gig was good and we had the whole next day off to relax on the beach and sleep off our hangovers whilst sunbathing in the beautiful hot weather. This time Colette and I laid our towels out first, a quiet spot closer to the water than before, less crowded, only sea and sand to look at. Wendi joined us as well, in a brand new swimsuit and clutching a small jar of Body Shop coconut sunscreen. Mr Vom, McGuire, Clive and our crew joined us throughout the day, wandering off from time to time to explore the seaside attractions and visit the bar, but Colette and I, covered in high factor sun block, stayed until sunset. And so did the chalky-skinned Wendi West.

I first noticed that Wendi was sunburnt early in the afternoon; she smeared some more pitifully ineffective moisturising grease over her angry, raw skin.

'I'll be fine,' she said, 'Body Shop only use natural ingredients.'

By the end of the day we had each caught the sun to some extent; a few red noses were noticeable but otherwise we were fine. Back at the hotel we prepared to leave for a night ferry back to England. As we packed we could hear screams, blood-curdling shrieks, relentless, never-ending cries of terrible, searing pain. Wendi was sitting in a cold bath, shaking with shock, like a lobster covered in ketchup, she was red, a deep, fierce, profound, flaming red.

'The worst sunburn,' the emergency doctor said, that he'd ever seen.

We had a laugh, on the night crossing, as we gambled in the ferry casino, happy on lager and nicely tanned. Wendi was in her bunk, pumped full of industrial strength tranquillisers (with no natural ingredients). Mr Vom didn't want to sleep; he wanted to watch the band that was advertised as playing in the bar, The Business. He hoped that they were the seventies Oi-punk band with the same name - but they turned out to be a cruise liner covers band.

'Nothing wrong with cover versions,' we joked as we watched.

We didn't need much sleep, there was another full day to recover at home before the next item on our busy schedule; we were shooting the video for *Burn*.

33. Colette

When Sue Hopkins announced her intended departure from the band...

'You don't know what goes on in my head,' she croaked dramatically, the news was met (much to her annoyance) with great indifference. This despite the fact that she had sung on every recording that the band had made since signing to IRS, including the album and *Spirit in the Sky*, but the opportunity to involve new, and possibly more attractive, blood was highly exciting. We instructed Jenny Cotton to place an advert in the classified section of Melody Maker, candidates for the position to be auditioned a week later.

The days of Clive inviting women that he fancied to join the band were long over; he was together with Wendi now, and she would be having none of it. I expressed an opinion that we should recruit someone who could actually sing, not just some hippie chic. We expected many attractive young Medics fans to apply for the post; Melody Maker was considered the 'inky' of choice for rock'n'roll vacancies, and we penned an advert to suit. Unfortunately, however, Jenny Cotton in her ultimate wisdom decided to place the advert in the theatrical publication The Stage. We had two applicants, neither of whom had heard of the band. Instead of the planned auditions in a plush rehearsal room, they were held at McGuire's flat in downtown Deptford, in his bedroom, with crusty tissues lying around the bed. Wendi went through some simple vocal parts with the two conservatively dressed stage school hopefuls, accompanied by McGuire on acoustic guitar, whilst Clive and I subjected them to 'interview' style interrogations in the living room. They couldn't have been more unsuitable if they'd tried, and they really couldn't sing.

Craig Duffy was a nice guy who worked for scary concert promoter John Curd and sometimes crewed for us. Duffy's girlfriend at the time was a smartly dressed, attractive but brassy blonde woman, appearing to be in her mid-thirties, who sometimes showed up backstage (a drink in one hand, cigarette in the other). A third candidate arrived at McGuire's flat, pre-arranged between Duffy and Wendi; it was Duffy's girlfriend, the middle-aged lady; her name was Colette. Clive and I listened in disbelief to her strong, powerful and accurate voice, she could sing. And when we chatted to her afterwards it transpired that (once changed from her office clothes and caked in fewer layers of Max Factor) she was in fact a saucy nineteen-year-old stunner with good bones, generous lips, flashing eyes and a body to die for, who was steeped in the rock'n'roll lifestyle and up for anything and everything. She got the job instantly.

Colette did come with one slight downside, her laugh. She laughed like a drain. An old, rusty metal drain clogged with bacon grease and rotten leaves - that was being played like a giant trombone by a braying donkey - amplified by a megaphone - along the Blackwall Tunnel. She was loud; loud like thunder in a biscuit tin. Like a pack of hounds fighting over pork chops. Shockingly, ear-splittingly, earth-quakingly muscular and manly, her laugh was ungodly in its volume and depth. But we loved her.

She joined the band in time to appear in the video for *Spirit In The Sky*, and we continued to tour exhaustively, internationally as well as domestically. Colette looked and sounded perfect, and she settled right in. Her first studio session was singing on the single *Burn,* so she was looking forward to the video shoot, looking slim, sun-kissed and gorgeous.

With faces rosy from our weekend spent on the beach in Holland, we arrived at the studio for the video shoot. Dressed in shades of scarlet, crimson and black, we matched the stage set, the scalding, steaming, fiery reds and burning flames of hell. Filmed posturing on our knees within a ring of fire that melted my spandex flares, plus the obligatory stage performance shots, the video had a dubious story line. The four Medics board a lift and travel downwards into hell, to be met, not by the devil, but by twenty

Anadin Brothers (an echo of the Hammersmith Palais bunch). Christian Paris and his brother, made-up and dressed to look like Wendi, were just two of the ugliest female backing singers ever captured on videotape.

During a break in filming, a brief respite from performing under the hot studio lamps, an emergency doctor was rushed in to treat Wendi's chronic sunburn. He prescribed the suffering Anadin Brother with a pack of paracetamol and advised that she didn't wear heavy clothing. She scraped the heavy, scratchy, glitter threaded stage costume back over her calamine lotion doused body, yelling and swearing. Profanities, disgusting and crude - and the only things louder than Colette's laugh.

34. Egg

As well as spiking my beer with paralysing alcohols, the band enjoyed a variety of time-filling and futile practical jokes. The most often practised was simply known as 'The Joke'. This consisted of driving the van away before the last band member had a chance to board... and that's it really. The van driver would drive a short distance... we'd wait until the victim (usually Mr Vom) was within arm's distance from the van door and then drive off again. This process would be repeated several times until we became bored. It passed the time.

Hiding clothes was one of Clive's favourite amusements. He threw away my things after a performance in Scotland; they were eventually discovered in a dustbin some weeks later. Another time, whilst changed into my pink crushed velvet catsuit, Clive hid my clothes, and I was forced to wear some workmen's overalls that I found in a skip. On one occasion in Italy, Clive didn't even wait until I'd changed out of my clothes before confiscating them. I was set upon by Colette and Wendi, intent on stripping me naked in the back of a tour bus as it pulled up at the doors of our hotel; meanwhile Clive and Mr Vom pinned me down with sturdy wrestler's grips. I kicked and struggled as they punched my hands and bit my fingers, desperately clinging onto my trousers as they wrenched them from my body. They eventually got the better of me, and I was stranded in the bus totally naked, my clothes stolen. I was faced with the humiliating prospect of walking from the bus, naked, entering the posh hotel, naked, negotiating for my door key with the Italian receptionist, naked, and then making my way to the room, totally stark bollock naked.

Fortunately, Clive forgot to take my jacket; a small red leather 'Levis' style jacket that had been tossed to the back of the bus, with my hotel door key still in the pocket. Dressed in nothing but this short, revealing garment (pulled down around my kidneys), key in hand, I sprinted from the bus, cock swinging in the breeze, through the street, across the road, through the swing doors, across the lobby, past the people in the lobby, through reception, into the lift, out of the lift, down the corridor and into my hotel room. Wendi returned my clothes later that evening.

I tried in vain to exact some kind of revenge on the perpetrators of my attack. I put 'farting powder' in their champagne... but no-one noticed. I put various joke-shop trickeries into their cigarettes, noisy explosives and exploding 'snow storm' gizmos; these just caused alarm in the expensive restaurant where I utilised them; the poor restaurant owner in tears, running around in a panic as feathery fake snow clouded his restaurant, spoiling his customers' food.

I did manage, however, to get my own back on the impish Mr Vom. Once, he was strutting around an Italian hotel room, entertaining his audience; naked, clucking, pretending to be a chicken, a fresh raw egg carefully clenched between his buttocks. I rushed up and kicked the egg from behind. It shot straight up Mr Vom's anus, whereupon he leaped two feet into the air. The eggshell broke up his arse, the yellow yolk dripping from its murky depths. As he hopped about in shock, his foot slipped on the dribbled egg yolk, and he somersaulted backwards, stubbing his toe on the metal bed frame and landing in an eggy tangled mess on his mattress.

'Well done, Dickie Damage,' he said pragmatically, rubbing his injured toe, 'we're evens.'

35. Wogan

When you are a loyal fan, when you follow and embrace a band, clutch it to your bosom as your very own; you may to some extent share the excitement and exhilaration of the band's success, witnessing something which you've helped create, something special, something that sets you apart from the crowd. Medics' fans were exactly that, passionate and true, proud to be part of a movement, of a scene; they were the 'out-crowd'.

The Medics fans put *Spirit In The Sky* in the charts, and the media hype did the rest. We expected the same thing to happen with *Burn*. The single was played heavily on the radio prior to the official release date, and the *Burn* video was shown on the usual music video slots, the ITV 'Chart Show' and a few others. Come the week of release our audience, still feeling part of the whole Medics, Alice In Wonderland, strange folk taking over the world euphoria, rushed to the shops and bought the record. It went straight in at number twenty-nine. The 'Top Of The Pops' chart had two Medics singles in its countdown at the same time, a truly great feeling. We just needed the single to get top twenty, and then we'd be invited back on TOTP. The Medics fans had done their bit, and now it was time for the media hype. But there was a glitch in the system, a cruel twist of fate that came from within, a streak of ruinous insanity that would alter the course of our lives forever and for the worse.

The record label had some fantastic news; they were very excited. Andrew King called us in for a meeting to share it with us, he too was very pleased. The TV pluggers had done us proud. In the mid-eighties, other than TOTP, the best possible television programme to present your single to the largest potential audience was the BBC teatime chat show Wogan. Everyone watched Wogan; it was huge. The much-coveted music slot on Wogan would almost certainly guarantee any record a top five chart position. Andrew King waited until we were all seated and settled before telling us the news; Jenny Cotton put down her lipstick and took the phones off the hook - silence.

'We've got Wogan,' he said in his finest speaking voice.

The room erupted with celebratory woops and cheers.

'YES! Hurrah, hooray, FUCKING YEEESSSSS!'

Beer cans flew through the air, grins fixed on every face. Mr Vom jumped from chair to chair looking for an open window, Jenny popped a champagne cork, McGuire gave Colette a congratulatory kiss. Andrew shook my hand firmly and gave Clive a hug.

'Well done, everyone,' he said between sips of fizzy wine. 'I must call Tannett,' he laughed, 'he wanted to tell you himself, but that my privilege, I get to spread the love.'

Jenny put the phones back on the hook, and it rang immediately, it was A&R man Steve Tannett.

'The label wants us to go round for a jolly-up,' Jenny beamed after taking the call.

We started gathering our things, draining beer and speed-quaffing champagne.

'Today should be good for another mega-IRS slap-up feed,' Andrew laughed, 'speeches and industry backslapping. We'll get Tannett to take us out for something nice and expensive, Japanese maybe. I hope everyone's hungry.'

However, there existed in that moment an element of brooding menace, one person in the room wasn't celebrating, one person wasn't smiling, wasn't happy; one solitary figure remained silent, lips pursed and arms tightly crossed throughout. One person was going nowhere, Wendi. She waited until, one by one, we'd calmed down, were on our feet, coats on and waiting to leave; the calm before the storm.

'I'm not fucking doing fucking Wogan,' she said adamantly.

We tried to appeal to Wendi, we begged her in fact, but she was resolutely stubborn, furious and frothing like a council-estate pit-bull.

'I had to go on fucking Top Of The fucking Pops when I didn't fucking want to, but I'm NEVER fucking going on fucking Wogan,' she spat at anyone brave enough to approach. Clive said nothing, he knew she wouldn't budge, gently shaking his head when Andrew asked for his intervention; it was pointless. The rest of us were heartbroken. Andrew relayed the bad news to Steve Tannett, who couldn't believe his ears.

'Was she mad?'
We sat heads in our hands, in shock, tearful and devastated.

'They'll do it without the girls,' Andrew offered in vain to the TV pluggers, but to no avail, they simply stopped working the record. That was that, they pulled the plug.

There was one other TV appearance which had been booked beforehand, the third division, hardly watched ITV children's television show called 'Razzmatazz', on which we half-heartedly mimed to a studio audience of primary school children. But without the TV pluggers' support, without the enthusiasm of the hype machine, the record got no higher in the charts than twenty nine, right where our faithful fans had originally put it. We missed out on TOTP, and *Burn* slipped from the charts and ultimately from people's memory.

36. Germany

The beer fridge in a German dressing room is always a
joy to behold; large, precisely cooled and packed to
bursting with delicious pilsner lager and syrupy Alt
beers; the tray of sliced cheese and meats which
usually accompanies, is tiny in comparison and often
untouched. The beer however was always finished. It
was after emptying the contents of one of these
marvellous refrigerators, having performed to a packed
and appreciative crowd, that we headed for McGuire's
hotel room. Word was that he'd managed to get two
girls back with him, and we wanted to see.

McGuire opened his door, Mr Vom, Colette
and I pushed passed and invaded his privacy; he did
indeed have two girls in his room and some wine, beer
and vodka. There were twin beds in his room, two
pretty punk girls were sitting on one, we sat on the
other facing them, McGuire stood between us
awkwardly, annoyed that we had interrupted. Mr Vom
immediately started his 'life of the party routine',
jumping about in his boxer shorts and smoking
cigarettes with his genitals. The young German girls
ignored McGuire, such was the quality of Mr Vom's
antics. McGuire desperately tried to re-attract their
attention, with little success. Colette produced a small
lump of hashish and some rolling papers and asked me
to skin up for her, I did so, using the palm of her hand
as 'my receptacle'. Colette and I flirted playfully and
got stoned whilst McGuire was reduced to futile
measures to grab the girls' attention away from Mr

Vom; gulping large swigs of neat vodka. We encouraged him and pretended to join in. After a couple of rounds of Swig and Swap, McGuire toppled over and passed out on a bed, which entertained us immensely, the pretty German girls also.

After sticking cigarette butts up McGuire's nostrils, we scribbled over his face with Colette's eyeliner and wrote profanities across his forehead, plus John Lennon spectacles, a neat goatee beard and a Hitler moustache. Shaving foam was next, sprayed over his cheeks in carefully applied ice cream spirals, some more cigarette butts added as 99 flakes. He looked great, the young girls found him hilarious, as did we.

The hashish finished, the drink gone, it was time to call it a night. We rolled McGuire onto his side so that he wouldn't choke on his own vomit, and shut the door behind us. I unlocked my door, but before retiring I helped Mr Vom stagger down the corridor to his room. Colette wandered in behind me as I returned to my room and closed the door.

'Do you still want me to be your receptacle?' she joked as we entered.
I stopped in my tracks; the two German girls were sitting on the edge of a bed.

'What are you doing, Dickie?' Colette asked as I sat between the girls with a stupid grin on my face.

'I'm going to bed,' I said, 'in this room, with two girls in it.'
Colette turned around and walked out.

'Goodnight, Dickie,' she said curtly.
The girls disappeared into the bathroom as I quickly undressed, dimmed the lights and got in one of the twin beds. I could hear giggling from the bathroom, they were taking their time. The elder of the two (mid-

length curly hair with a pear shaped figure) appeared
from the bathroom first. She'd stripped to her pink bra,
tights pulled up over her knickers, a little frumpy but
still sexy. She climbed into the bed next to mine; I'd
dragged the twin beds together in preparation. The
other girl was prettier, with spiky black Siouxsie Sioux
hair and make-up. She appeared in a black lace bra,
matching knickers, stockings and suspenders and
climbed into the bed next to her friend. I could not
believe my luck. The curly haired one moved over and
stroked my cheek.

'Zank you for letting us stay,' she purred.
I leant in and kissed her, rolling on top as our tongues
locked into a full-on wet snog, my hand tackling her
American tan pantyhose.

'Hey,' said the other girl.
I shifted my weight and kissed the second girl, my free
hand exploring her lingerie, my remaining palm still
secure in the other's elasticated tights.

Now, there was nothing in this universe that
I'd ever wanted, hoped for, dreamt of, prayed for, as
much as being with two girls at once, and now, due to
McGuire's unconsciousness (and Mr Vom's superior
revelry) two lady-punks were in my arms. I thanked
every god that happened to be listening. I removed the
younger one's bra, incredible, I caught myself
laughing with disbelief. This was going to be the
greatest night of my life.

At this point things began to go terribly wrong.
They stopped kissing me and started to chat; the
discussion became quite heated. As I attempted to
remove more underwear they argued. I felt a suspender
belt snap from my fingers as they jumped out of bed
and returned to the bathroom. I could hear them

spitting language at each other for what seemed like an eternity.

'We do not do zis,' the older one said on their return.

I shook my head slowly, suspecting the worst.

'You must choose,' she said.

'No, both at once,' I begged, 'please.'

They sat on the bed and kissed me, the eldest first; she pulled away and stood up. The younger one next, I grabbed her, I'd made my choice. She rolled in between the sheets as the other moved to the twin bed. But, stupidly, I didn't give up; as I focused my affections on the pretty girl underneath me, I surreptitiously explored next to us, my fingers working and within. The moans from her friend alerted my companion to my actions; she threw me off, sat up and launched into an endless rant. Disappointment and fatigue got the better of me and I finally succumbed to sleep whilst the two friends bickered.

I was woken at dawn as they left. As they kissed me goodbye, I attempted a last minute seduction, but to no avail.

'You always want fucky fucky,' the younger girl complained as she pulled herself away. They left without fucky fucky, and I was, and always will be, gutted.

37. Playback

The Italian 'playback concert' is the music festival
equivalent of an orgasm, an involuntary spasm of ego,
ecstasy and monkey business. A perk of chart success;
an invitation to perform before a packed sport stadium
of admiring pop fans, without having to actually play a
single note; you never need be sober - and you get
paid. A conveyor belt of pop stars; wined and dined
from the moment they are landed at the airport,
ushered onto a stage, illuminated by a humongous
lighting rig shining through a fog bank of dry ice; a
few minutes spent miming to a record or two, then
whisked away to more restaurants, bars and nightclubs
(the expensive kind). Plus a luxury hotel room to grab
a couple of hours sleep before the return flight.
Throughout the long Italian summers, we mimed along
to *Spirit In The Sky* and *Burn*, spoilt by first-class
hospitality, high on life and exquisitely pissed.

The screaming audience didn't seem to care
what we did on stage; we mimed atrociously, waving
arms and drumsticks randomly in hit-or-miss time to
the music, dancing out of step and out of our heads.
On one occasion the girls forgot to pack their wigs.

'We don't fucking perform without our wigs,'
Wendi spat at the poor Italian stage manager. Colette
was too hammered to care. The audience didn't notice
and went crazy as the female backing vocals and dance
routines were performed by an empty space full of
blue smoke.

If the antics on stage looked too anarchic, the lighting men simply flooded the stage with even more dry ice; sometimes I couldn't see Mr Vom for the clouds of thick acrid fog, other than the occasional flash of red crimped hair or flailing wooden stick.

Clive was on one occasion so paralytic that he tripped over his cumbersome cape at the very moment of his stage entrance at the summit of a massive staircase. He waved to the audience then fell arse over tit, tumbling clumsily down the Perspex steps, thump, thump, thump. He sprang to his feet and signalled a mighty thumbs-up to the crowd, a symbol of victorious effort over alcohol, only to trip and fall awkwardly down the remaining staging, clump, clump, clump, until he finally hit the bottom, hard, the dry ice partially masking his gangly legs knotted between the folds of tangled velvet. Chrissie Hynde of The Pretenders watched Clive's drunken acrobatics from the side of the stage in utter bewilderment; some bands remained professionally sober. These events were usually televised throughout mainland Europe, as we discovered later.

It was after one of these marvellous shows that I fell in love with Hollywood actress Brooke Shields, or so I assumed; the day started as it ended, strangely. We shared the flight over with the hydraulically breasted Brigitte Nielsen; we whispered behind her seat that breast implants explode at high altitude; she seemed anxious and requested that the flight attendants check that the plane wasn't flying too high. After we'd booked into our hotel rooms, quaffed several chilled lagers, mimed to a couple of records in front of a vast stadium crowd, ate a delicious meal accompanied by delicious wine, we boarded a bus and headed for the local exclusive nightclub, inexplicably named Hollywood International Airport. Bridget Nielsen was in the VIP area, nervously examining her gigantic plastic boobs. The bar was expensive but free for us; we ordered champagne and bottled beer. Clive was leaning against the bar, head sagging worryingly, vomiting over people's shoes. Mr Vom handed me four bottles of cold lager, which I carefully placed into the pockets of my leather army coat. As the ornate bar flooring began to flood with spilt champagne and stomach bile, I noticed a vision of unspeakable beauty standing opposite; with eyes stunning and bright, with lustrous auburn hair that shone under the lights and rosebud lips and perfect dazzling white teeth. She smiled and said hello in a soft Californian accent.

'It's Brooke Shields,' I shouted in Mr Vom's ear, tugging at the shoulder of his banana yellow jumpsuit.

'No, it's not,' Vom replied, adamantly.
I took hold of Brooke's lovely hand and followed her along the edge of the dance floor, introducing myself as we walked. We stood in a darkened corner, face to face. I expressed my undivided attention, a passionate belief in love at first sight, how young she looked in real life and the brilliance of her acting roles. She laughed gently as I poured my heart out; she'd noticed the crotch of my trousers, it was soaking wet, as were my legs. Mr Vom had turned the bottles upside down in my pockets as I followed Brooke through the club. Her friends giggled as I told them of my devotion to her and asked if they were American actresses too; none of them were. They insisted that they were Italian and that she wasn't Brooke Shields at all, as did Brooke Shields. She claimed to be a student on an exchange trip.

Mr Vom appeared and said we were leaving before they threw Clive out for puking on the dance floor. I pulled Brooke with me out into the humid night air; her friends followed, grasping her other hand, trying to prevent me from dragging her into the bus.

'Really, I'm not Brooke Shields,' she insisted unconvincingly.

We were wrenched apart by her friends and Mr Vom. I waved goodbye through the tinted window, she smiled sweetly whilst her friends laughed heartily.

'But I love her,' I protested as the tour bus pulled away.

'She's not fucking Brooke Shields, Dickie,' Colette moaned as I continued my lament.

Back at the hotel Mr Vom put a small brown button in my mouth that I assumed was chocolate.

'Swallow this, Dickie Damage,' he said. It was a tiny lump of hashish. 'It'll cheer you up.'

Bags already packed, I left my door slightly ajar and sat up through the night in Mr Vom's room; discussing the unfathomable rules of love, the odds of meeting Hollywood actress Brooke Shields in an Italian nightclub (coincidentally named Hollywood) and the lengths that she took to remain unrecognised.

I finally retired to my room to grab an hour's sleep before our morning call for the return flight - only to spend sixty minutes re-packing my bag. Clive had unpacked every item of clothing from my luggage; he'd carefully folded and tidied them away within the drawers, cupboards and hard to find corners of the room. My toiletry bag was emptied, the contents neatly placed in a long line directly under the bathroom mirror. The hashish busy in my bloodstream, I pawed away at the mirror and its reflections, my toiletries many, massive and oddly...

just...
out of...
reach.

38. Mission

Sometimes you are given the opportunity to play on some really odd bills, peculiar line-ups with a mix-match of artists, the concerts of the strange. One such bizarre musical assortment was at the Crystal Palace Bowl featuring, amongst others, us, Hawkwind, Spear Of Destiny, The Enid, Balaam and The Angel, The March Violets, Comsat Angels, and Second World War darling Vera Lynn. We all ran on stage to assist Vera perform her encore, *The White Cliffs Of Dover*; punks, Goths and piss-heads united in a ridiculous mass sing-song to encourage sobriety and raise awareness of drug abuse; with Clive speeding off his nut and Mr Vom sitting on my shoulders swigging a litre of cider. The hapless concert security guards squeezed themselves into small rubber dinghies, splashing fitfully around the moat in front of the stage as various drugged-up nutters tried to doggy-paddle across the filthy water to touch the hem of Vera's evening dress. Vera wasn't intimidated and seemed to enjoy herself, a true pro.

These more eccentric concert events didn't always have a happy outcome; one in particular had unfortunate consequences. We were booked to play the San Siro Stadium in Milan with another weird running order. Indi-radio favourites - Red Lorry Yellow Lorry, ex-Sisters Of Mercy rockers - The Mission, wacky pop hippies - Doctor and the Medics, 77 originators - The Damned, queens of punk rock glamour - Siouxsie and the Banshees, and, to headline the entire festival of alternative music, suave American big-band showman - Kid Creole and The Coconuts. The event was great, the audience enthusiastic and the performances good. Despite the clash of styles; Kid Creole was especially brilliant, his band professional and tight. They were the best band of the day.

The Coconuts didn't attend the post-gig piss-up in the small bar opposite the hotel; the promoter had wisely booked them into a different establishment miles away from the noisy rock'n'roller types. Everyone was fairly merry, but numbers began to dwindle as the early hours approached; small groups decanted back to the hotel for nightcaps, leaving only a handful of musicians drinking in the bar including Rat Scabies, Clive and a few others. Mr Vom went to bed; McGuire and I opened a last bottle of Peroni in Colette's room, we weren't planning on a 'late one' as we had an early start next morning. The calm of Colette's room was suddenly shattered by loud thumping, the door rattled in its frame, and a generic picture shook from the flimsy studded wall. McGuire opened the door, and a furious long-haired Northerner rushed towards the bed, swearing blue murder and brandishing a bottle of vermouth.

'I fookin' kill you fookin' Doctor and the fookin Medics,' he shouted at my face.
I ducked under a swinging Martini bottle and darted after McGuire - who was already sprinting down the corridor away from the danger zone.
I heard footsteps chasing behind me and Colette slamming her door. McGuire opened our door and disappeared inside. I managed to just scrape inside the room as McGuire locked the door hard behind me. We barricaded the door with our guitar flight cases, the irate drunkard battering the outside with heavy fists.

The ruckus eventually faded, moving back down the corridor, coming to a halt a few rooms away, where it renewed its attack with fresh vigour on Mr Vom's door. Rudely woken from his precious slumber, Mr Vom opened his door to investigate the commotion. He was greeted by an aggressive swearing man who he promptly punched in the nose and returned to bed.

The next morning we learnt that the noisy Northerner was Craig Adams, the bassist from The Mission, and the motive for his torrent of fury was an incident in the bar. Rat Scabies had, as was often his penchant, fallen into an argument with Craig. Harmless at first, some light ribbing over the North/South divide, which unfortunately progressed into insults, at which point Clive became involved. Finally bored with the subject Scabies left the bar and Clive followed - but as Clive walked from the building he slapped Craig around the face, hands clad in heavy silver jewellery; then he delivered one final stupid jibe, announcing with the authority and hindsight of a man who'd just had a cover version hyped to Number One, a remark that would return to haunt him forever after...

'You'll never amount to anything in the music business,' he sneered.

Recently formed from various members of Gothic rockers Sisters Of Mercy, guitarist Wayne Hussey assembled The Mission with ex-Sisters bassist Craig Adams, and they were subsequently signed to a seven-album deal with Mercury Records. They released the debut album *God's Own Medicine*, which awarded them with several hit singles, a coveted gold disc and massive worldwide sales. Many albums followed, selling in large quantities to an ever expanding and fiercely loyal fan base. As Wayne

Hussey became famous, a rock star whose opinion was frequently expressed on the radio and in the music papers and pop magazines, he bad-mouthed Doctor and the Medics at every possible opportunity.

39. New York

Packing for a six-week long tour of America requires considerable planning and serious luggage. I settled on the largest nylon holdalls that London's Brick Lane market had to offer and purchased two of them, one for stage clothes and another for everything else. They were incredibly cumbersome and heavy; a fact that Clive enjoyed exploiting, calling my hotel room whilst I was still asleep and adopting a generic hotel front desk accent to inform me that...

'The band is waiting in the van ready to leave, Sir.'

I'd rush from my room stressed and hung over, half asleep and half-dressed, dragging two weighty bags, only to discover an empty van parked somewhere far along the road or at the furthest corner of a parking lot, the rest of the band still in bed obviously. I fell for this in America twice... and at least once in Italy.

The tour was a strenuous New York to Los Angeles and back-again slog that took in all of the major cities and a token gig in Canada; during which nerves were worn, hearts were broken, we featured in a Hollywood movie and Mr Vom caught Legionnaires' disease. Andrew King, assuming his finest Englishman abroad persona, joined us, as did our usual road crew, TM Martin Pyle, Roadie Welsh Carl and Soundman Harry D'mac, all of whom were fit and fresh, as were we, but by the end every one of us was ruined and rinsed.

The promoter provided us with a native New Yorker 'translator' to show us around and keep us from getting killed, a big-hearted Hawaiian shirt-wearing man named John Butler, who had previously worked for our new friends Kid Creole and The Coconuts. He took us to the trendiest bars and night clubs, a neon disco palace called The Palladium (where we would play a month later), the original converted church venue The Limelight, an uber-fashionable neon box called the Milk Bar and our favourite bohemian dive, The Kit Kat club, where we watched New York new wave groups and drank bourbon and Tia Maria cocktails called Rusty Nails.

Jet-lagged and hungry, our first night in town started with food. We were joined in a lively Cajun restaurant by fellow British band General Public (the new group formed by Dave Wakeling and Rankin Roger of Two-Tone combo The Beat). We drank white rum cocktails from skull-shaped cups and ate jerk chicken and spicy meat-filled pastries. It all looked delicious, but unfortunately I couldn't taste the food. I'd accepted a five dollar bet with Mr Vom that I could eat a pasty doused in hot sauce. I put my five bucks on the table. Mr Vom did the same and shook several drops of chilli sauce over the pastry, and then so did Rankin Roger and Clive, who emptied the entire bottle over the plate. I won fifteen dollars, but my mouth felt like I'd poured in molten tarmac. Roger and Wakeling declined our offer to come drinking with us after the promoter paid the large bill, but they promised to hook up before they left town. They waved goodbye as we drove away in stretch limousines to explore the city nightlife. We never met them again.

We hung out in New York for a few days to acclimatise before our first gig at The Roxie, a famous old music hall venue where everyone who was anyone had played. Packed full of New York's hipsters, swingers and people in the know, this show was crucial to our success in the States. This was to be the fifth time that I fell over on stage, or, more precisely, was thrown over. Clive crawled through my legs during the encore, hoisting me up to his full height, stomping about the stage whilst we played *Silver Machine*. Heaving me skywards from his shoulders, he jumped from between my legs, and I fell backwards onto my back, from where I finished the song.

The crowd went crazy for us, the set was powerful and Clive worked the audience brilliantly; they lapped up his cheesy theatrics. But when we came off stage my back was hurting badly, and I crawled into an empty dressing room to lie quietly on the floor. A friend of the band, and a renowned music journalist, Kris Needs, walked into the dressing room to discover his cute mini-skirted girlfriend straddling my back and massaging my shoulders whilst I gently moaned with relief. It must have looked compromising because he stormed out, she chased after him pleading innocence. I got the impression that America was going to be gruelling and complicated.

40. McGuire

How McGuire managed to attract any women at all
was an absolute mystery to most people. A man so
unhygienic that having once leant him some shoes for
a video shoot, a few hours later, they smelt so badly
that they had to be destroyed. An individual so miserly
and tight that he was nicknamed Captain Bargain
(regarding his preference for the cheap things in life
and the lengths taken to find them). I left my bass
guitar at his flat, a convenience for song-writing; he
sold it. He was a sleazy, scruffy, occasionally whiffy
man with the dress sense of a sack of potato peelings,

but he did get the girls. The beautiful Justine from Newcastle being a case in point; she was stunning. When once asked how he 'pulled' such beautiful women, his reply was simple and ruthless...

'I wear them down.'

McGuire would keep on and on and on and on, until the girl of his affections simply gave way and let him have his foul fetid pleasures. This tactic was put straight to work on Colette, and eventually, incredibly, it worked.

The morning after 'the fight with The Mission' Mr Vom, Colette and I hired a Fiat Panda and drove off into the Italian mountains with McGuire at the wheel. During a fun-filled week, staying with a distant cousin of Colette (who she'd previously never met) and his family (none of whom could speak English) we managed to upset the entire village community.

Once the initial shock from having to house and feed three unexpected English musicians, as well as Colette, had subsided, the simple Italian family relaxed slightly and sat with arms folded, waiting to be entertained. I juggled a bit, Mr Vom stuck cigarettes in his ears and McGuire goofed about and tried to touch Colette's leg. We were taken to a local disco where the DJ played *Spirit In The Sky;* and to a mountain lake where locals sunbathed topless and where McGuire goofed around and tried to touch Colette's leg. We were taken up a mountain ravine to watch hang-glider pilots throwing themselves from the highest peaks; and where Mr Vom discovered that he suffers from vertigo and tried to jump from the cable car. We were given antipasti and cherries marinated in brandy by a man with a permanently sozzled smile, and wafer-thin pizza cooked in a red brick oven by a humongous chef that specialised in tiny foods; meanwhile McGuire goofed about and tried to touch Colette's leg.

We were presented each morning with a wonderful breakfast feast of meats, breads and cheeses, which became slightly less wonderful each day as they tired of our ungrateful behaviour and ravenous appetite. Then, once the disturbance at the beer festival involving Mr Vom, the yodelling man's fiancé and the Italian police had run its course, the plate of delicious delicatessen treats vanished completely. We understood that we had outstretched our already precarious welcome and left in search of safer adventures and for other opportunities in which McGuire could set about his amorous ambitions.

After a couple of days mooching around Venice we headed back to Milan where we had arranged to join with Martin Pyle for a flight back to London, but we had one last night on the town. We checked into a very reasonably priced two-star hotel (which turned out to be a brothel), got changed and headed for a suitable nightclub that we'd spotted nearby. We drank cocktails and danced to ZZ Top records, meanwhile McGuire steadily worked on Colette. Mr Vom and I sat in a booth and speed drank Gin Fizz, laughing at how squiffy we were getting. All the time McGuire worked his charms, dancing and goofing with Colette, trying it on, always joking, always touching. We passed away the warm small hours and made the most of our final night of holiday fun, but the club was soon to close.

We went to the bar one last time and ordered a final batch of Gin Fizz; the return met with utter disbelief. Our blood-shot eyes stung with salt from the sight of what awaited us, jealousy numbed our tongues as we stared in shock and silence. McGuire was kissing Colette, snogging with fevered tongues, his fingers stroking her thighs and running up and down her pretty legs. Finally, this time, she didn't slap them away.

41. L.A

Colette bored of McGuire's favours during the first few days in New York, at which point he took to walking round the hotel room, which he shared with me, naked and reading the bible. He stole a ubiquitous King James edition from a hotel drawer; everyone else stole pillows - to better sleep on the long bus journeys. He didn't really snap out of his 'religious phase' until he managed to pull an American groupie in Los Angeles; his wallet was stolen from the room that same day.

Our roadie, Welsh Carl, had a friend living in L.A., Lucy, a petite Mexican prostitute with braces on her teeth and a purse full of crystal meth. One morning Carl was lying by the hotel pool with soundman Harry D'mac; they hadn't been to bed. Harry was from the north of England. A small blond-haired man who liked his music loud but had quit working for all bands except for The Medics; and for this we loved him. Harry's claim to fame was that he'd turned off Paul McCartney's microphone during the first few bars of his performance on the Live Aid Wembley concert. He liked a drink and other stimulants, but on this particular Los Angeles morning, a gig day, his face had bloated from overindulgence. Acquiring the deep rusty hue normally reserved for long-term homeless alcoholics or the acutely sunburnt, his cheeks blotchy and swollen and with bulging burgundy eye-balls, he couldn't talk other than for a few one-syllable words...

'Get-t'-fook.' Or simply, 'fook.'

He managed to string some sentences together for the gig that evening, an outdoor family event in an LA suburb. We were only allowed a quick line-check to sort stage monitoring and the 'out front' sound through the PA system, whilst the audience was already in the field, watching us. Harry's mixing desk was a long way from the stage, he needed to communicate with us, and for this reason he had a microphone plugged into his mixing desk. But he forgot to mute the 'out front' sound, so the audience could hear him through the speakers.

'My fookin' head is fookin' kill'n' me,' he said, to the horror of the family crowd.
Security guards and policemen flew into immediate action, running around trying to source the perpetrator of this offensive and illegal broadcast. Initially they ran on stage to check that it wasn't any of us, to no effect, they simply couldn't work out who else might have a microphone. Harry didn't care and continued his filthy dialogue.

'Why don't those fookin' policemen stop sniffin' round your fookin' arse, get off that fookin' stage so that we can get on with the fookin' sound-check!'
The actual gig was great. Harry didn't get arrested by the LAPD, and he celebrated that evening in a similar fashion to the previous night, courtesy of Lucy's purse.

The next evening we were to play in the L.A. Whisky a Go Go. Again, Harry's head looked like a giant swollen plumb. Clive was sent to do a radio interview to plug the gig early that afternoon. To his dismay, a caller phoned into the station and to say that...

'The subject matter of *Spirit In The Sky* and the demonic hair-style on the single sleeve clearly indicate that The Doctor is a Satan worshipper, if not the Devil himself,' and that during the concert that evening...

'I intend to shoot him.'

Clive appeared at the sound-check, pale and terrified, clearly believing every word of the anonymous caller, certain that he was to be shot dead in a crazy Lennon/Kennedy style assassination. We, however, assumed that it was just a prank call and ignored it.

Whilst we ate burritos in a restaurant before the show, a journalist for *Rolling Stone* magazine interviewed Clive for a short feature. The interviewer, coincidentally, was an old school acquaintance of Clive's; he too wasn't very impressed with the 'death threat', which was the only thing that Clive wanted to talk about during the interview. We watched as questions were ignored and eyes glazed over.

The gig, it transpired, was fine. Clive adopted an even more Elvis-esque American accent and ended each song with a sincere...

'God Bless!'

There was, however, one dramatic incident during the show - somebody threw an ice cube at him.

42. Toupee glue

Everyone had bad hair in the eighties, it was the fashion; we were lost without our hair-driers. Mine at the time, in retrospect, looked like a hat, an Irish Guard's bear-skin in fact. I didn't realise that it looked ridiculous, because everyone else had 'big' hair; I thought that I looked normal. Every day, whilst Mr Vom sat cross-legged crimping his hair straight enough to spike into shape, I would be performing similar unmanly beautifications.

My barnet was a back-combed bouffant, stiff with hair lacquer and gel but with one extra added affectation, I had, as was peculiar to certain mod hair-cuts, long 'sidey' bits. Instead of sideburns, I grew long sections of hair down the side of my face, which were styled into oversized kiss-curls and shaped around my cheek-bones. Already thick with dried hair products, once blow-dried into shape, I secured these wings to the sides of my face with spirit gel, or to use the street vernacular, toupee glue. A brown viscous liquid that, when applied to the head with a small brush, dries clear. Formulated to stick men's wigs to their bald heads, it was another idea of my girlfriend Madeleine.

The glue worked fairly well, it was invisible and pretty strong, except for when I started to sweat, upon which the wings would un-stick from my face and flap around in the air. I developed a habit of fiddling with the unattached flaps, rolling them between my fingers, picking the glue from between the strands, removing a little more hair each time. I started the American tour with perfect thick kiss-curls framing my face; by halfway through they'd thinned down to a fraction of their former glory, spirally little twizzles of gluey hair matted to my ears. People often mistook me for a Hasidic Jew - wearing a funny hat.

43. Movie

Whilst in L.A., we were invited to appear in a Hollywood movie, playing 'the band' in a nightclub scene. The movie was called *Maid To Order*, telling the tale of a spoilt rich girl who is 'magically' forced to seek employment as a housemaid. Starring eighties 'Brat Pack' actress Ally Sheedy, known for her roles in *The Breakfast Club*, *St Elmo's Fire*, *War Games* and *Short Circuit*. She was well-known and cute. It necessitated extending the tour for a couple of extra days, to which Wendi objected, but Andrew King talked her round, 'we needed the money'.

It was a one-day shoot with a very early start, filmed in a large venue next to one of the studio lots in Universal City. We came with our own costumes and make-up, so we didn't need to be there so early. We killed time by hanging around the catering department, eating breakfast burgers, star spotting and enjoying the Anadin Brothers being mistaken for men. Finally, it was call time.

The filming itself consisted of us miming along to *Spirit In The Sky*, high up on stage, in front of a hundred movie extras 'going wild'. They filmed from every conceivable angle. Then we stopped for lunch. After which they shot individual band members, miming along to *Spirit In The Sky*, from every possible angle whilst the audience danced energetically, and then we broke for dinner. Then they filmed Ally Sheedy dancing amongst the 'enthusiastic' crowd, whilst we mimed along to *Spirit In The Sky* in the background. They shot from every angle, and then we broke for supper. Then they filmed Ally Sheedy on stage with us, dancing next to the Anadin Brothers, failing to copy their choreography, whilst the crowd whooped and we mimed along to *Spirit In The Sky*. They shot from every conceivable angle possible, and then, finally, they finished for the day. It took forever.

We feature in the finished movie for a few short seconds, fairly close to the beginning. I have never watched the whole thing.

44. Bucket

The Munich Hilton was a classy German hotel with many bars in which we had, on one occasion, a whole evening to enjoy. We settled in a modest looking disco bar with an illuminated dance floor and sparkly lights that flicked around the black flock wallpaper from a small spinning glitter ball. We looked completely at odds with the handful of seventies-suited clientele strutting about to Madonna's latest album, but we successfully purchased beer from the bar, sat politely at the far end (the whole band and road crew, plus Andrew King) and tried to not attract attention. The bar staff looked slightly concerned but relaxed when

Harry D'mac purchased an expensive bottle of champagne, nestled in a giant brimming silver ice bucket.

The atmosphere was mellow, the alcohol was flowing, and we were all enjoying ourselves. Our young monitor man, Stephan (sadly now deceased) started dancing with some Turkish businessmen, Colette also. Harry finished his champagne and returned the empty bottle back to the bar in the huge shiny bucket, whereupon it was refilled with fresh ice and a second bottle resting on the top. He could barely carry the bucket such was its weight, spilling ice cubes across the carpet as he staggered back to our table. The beer was constantly flowing, as well as the fizz, and spirits were high. Colette grew bored of dancing; the Turkish businessmen were becoming over-friendly, so she sat down. Stephan, as a result, started thrusting himself up against the randy Turks, rubbing his crotch and grabbing theirs. They left the dance floor soon after. The bar was all ours.

The second champagne bottle was emptied, and attentions focused on just how much ice was in the large gleaming bucket. Clive dared Mr Vom to stick his arse in it for one minute, and we all laughed. But, in a flash, Mr Vom pulled down his PVC trousers and plopped his bare arse into the mountain of ice, balls and all.

'Gaaahhh!' Mr Vom exclaimed, as the freezing ice burnt his testicles.
Tour Manager Martin Pyle counted sixty seconds on his watch, and Vom rolled off from the ice, his buttocks red and numb. Andrew King said goodnight at this point in the proceedings, he guessed what was going to happen. Mr Vom dared Clive to stick his arse in the ice for two minutes.

'Ahhh, I'm freezing my bollocks off,' Clive growled as his naked ball-sack chilled on the ice for two minutes, his competitive streak to the fore. Harry D'mac was next, for three minutes.

'Get, t'fookin' fook, fookin' freezing ma' fookin' noots,' he said.

The bucket was refilled to overflowing, the barman cooperating eagerly when fingers pointed towards Colette.

'Whaaaaaaaaaaaaaaaaaaaaaaaaaaaaaaaah,' Colette screamed, as she suffered her icy torture, and then so did McGuire, then Stephan and even Wendi. Martin Pyle, who was trying to avoid the issue by being the timekeeper, reluctantly yanked down his pants and endured the ordeal, teeth clenched and cheeks flushed; I sat quietly saying nothing, it was nearing my turn. To my great relief, Mr Vom insisted on having another go and splashed into the icy water for more. This was my chance to escape. I shifted to the edge of the sofa and crossed my legs as if in urgent need of the toilet. Colette noticed me edging away.

'Where are you off to, Dickie?' she cackled. 'It's your go next. We want to see your chilly willy.'

'I'm just gonna go for a quick leak, and then I'll be straight back to have my turn,' I lied, walking purposefully towards the toilet. Harry and Stephan rushed to the bar to refill the bucket with fresh bum-numbing ice cubes. I opened the toilet door as if to enter, then made my break.

'Get him!'

I sprinted from the toilet, out of the bar, across the hotel lobby and into the lifts. I watched nervously as the crazed cold-arsed rabble charged after me, Harry and Stephan dragging the heavy bucket between their legs, scattering ice cubes over the polished marble floor. The lift doors shut just in time. I burst out of the opening doors and down the corridor to my room, unlocked my door and shut it safely behind me.

'Richard... Richard, open the door!' McGuire was locked out; we were sharing the room.
I didn't trust him.

'Where are they?'

'They got off on the wrong floor, let me in, it's safe,' he insisted.
I put the door on the chain and peaked through for signs of the others. It was just McGuire outside, but I could hear the others closing in. I unchained the door and pulled McGuire through, locking the door securely behind us. A heartbeat later, the mob was at the door, banging, shouting and thumping.

'Open up.' They demanded, repeatedly. Bang! Bang! Bang! 'Open up, or we'll break it down.' Bang! Bang! Bang!
They began attacking the hinges and attempted to unscrew the lock with the screwdriver on a Swiss Army knife.

'I'm going to let them in,' McGuire said. 'They're going to break down the door.'
I locked myself into the bathroom and barricaded the door; wedging my back against the sink and pushing my feet against the handle. And then I waited. McGuire let them inside. I heard them storm into the room, I braced myself as the bathroom door rattled in its frame, they battered the door, thump, thump, thump! Voices, muffled and raised, a cacophony of cracking wood and drunken shouts, and then it went quiet. I strained my ears, nothing... ten minutes passed.

'They've gone,' McGuire eventually said through the door.

I emerged from my sanctuary to discover my bedding strewn around the room and the entire contents of the giant silver ice bucket dumped into the middle of my mattress, which was soaked and sagging under its watery weight.

We checked out the following morning, after a hearty continental breakfast, but the cleaners had already discovered my ruined mattress. Andrew King was deep in argument with the hotel manager as we left.

'Somebody hez wet ze bed. It must be paid for,' the irate manager hissed.
Andrew adopted his finest speaking voice and replied...

'My dear fellow, once you have had the liquid in the mattress properly analysed, which I'm confident is merely tap water, please notify me as to whether you find any traces of urine. If so, I'll gladly pay for a new one; until then, kindly fuck off.'

45. Japan

Supporting Alice Cooper was great; we got to watch
his set every night from a VIP box or private area
positioned high above or to the side of the stage. We
could see how he did many of his theatrical trickeries.
I shan't spoil 'the guillotine trick', but it's far less
impressive once you've seen it from the side.
We played with him twice, during his *The Nightmare
Returns* Tour, on the 23rd November at Wembley Arena
1986, and the 25th at The Edinburgh Playhouse.
Alice is a very nice man, despite his gruesome
persona, his favourite band is The Who (the same as
mine), he was a member of the legendary 70s hazing
club The Hollywood Vampires, with John Lennon,
Harry Nilsson and Keith Moon.
        His audience liked us, they could see his
influence in Clive's stage performance, and we were
offered a third concert, which we graciously turned
down. Death rockers (and ex-Batcavers) Alien Sex
Fiend gladly accepted the gig in our stead; we had a
prior engagement; we were off to Japan.

In each room of our plush Tokyo hotel we were gifted
with a large ornate porcelain barrel of Sake (Japanese
rice wine) served via a simple tap from the side of the
keg into tiny vessels that resembled eggcups. Best
consumed hot (to burn off some of the alcohol) cold
Sake tastes like fermented rubber. Mr Vom developed
quite a taste for it; he finished his keg by the second
day of our stay – so I gave him mine.

We were also given by the way of a present: guitars and basses (courtesy of Randy Fernandez), Kimonos, decorated bamboo fans, souvenir chop sticks, tea sets, t-shirts, painted lamps and lanterns, Kokeshi dolls, traditional scarves, masks, leather goods and lots and lots of fruit. Record company staff, tour promoters, press agents, journalists, anyone with access to a souvenir shop, insisted on showering us with trinkets, but this wasn't just the reserve of music industry personnel, fans did the same.

There would be a crowd of giggling fans outside every hotel and venue, following us through streets and shopping centres, loitering in hotel lobbies and bars, armed with bags of curiosities, all gifts for us. Mr Vom was a particularly popular target to shower with presents; he'd stagger around, his arms full with stuff; mostly from admiring girls, they shared something in common with the compact drummer - they were of a similar height. They knew his room number, and they all wanted to marry him. By the end of the Japanese tour, Vom was exhausted by this torrent of female attention; Harry D'mac tied a white handkerchief to a pole for Vom to wave as he walked through the hotel lobby, a symbolic gesture of surrender. He simply needed to get some rest.

One on occasion, after a few heavy nights, the band and crew were winding down in the hotel bar. A group of fashionable females sat a table away, clutching designer handbags, chatting between themselves but affording us occasional glances. The bar eventually shut, and one by one we left. Mr Vom invited me and McGuire to his room to share a bottle of decanted rum and coke. As we walked from the bar the women followed. When we navigated through the corridors they followed also. As we entered Mr Vom's room they followed directly behind. We sat in the room in disbelief, surrounded by thirteen smartly attired Japanese ladies, smiling, nodding and not speaking English. Dressed in the height of Tokyo trends (short pleated skirts, thigh socks, buckled boots and leather box jackets), the ladies accepted our meagre half empty plastic bottle of flat Bacardi and coke and laughed politely at Mr Vom's antics, but it was very late, we were tired, and the party was winding to a close. I said goodnight and left the others to it. The lady sitting to my side stood up and, uninvited, trailed behind and followed me into my room. I sat on my bed, beat and bewildered, but a woman in my room, I naturally reasoned, was a good thing. She was slim and a little taller than the twelve others; I guessed her to be in her mid to late twenties, early thirties at a push; her clothes looked expensive and immaculate. Her bobbed hairstyle was as perfectly executed as her make-up; the vivid blue hue of her pupils betrayed the cosmetic contact lenses in her eyes. I shook the fatigue from my mind and waited in eager anticipation of what might follow. Whereupon she bowed politely, removed her boots, pulled a blanket from her bag, laid it on the floor and went straight to sleep. This, it transpired, although highly perplexing and not a little disappointing at the time, was fortunate.

The following morning she was gone, but not before drawing me a bath, neatly folding my clothes and carefully packing my luggage. As we checked out of the hotel, we were mobbed for autographs by a familiar gaggle of sniggering females, there were thirteen of them. They hadn't gone home; those without a hotel room carpet on which to crash had slept in the lobby.

They didn't appear to be as mature in the morning light or without make-up, plus they had changed from their sophisticated designer clothes. They were all wearing school uniform.

46. Waterloo

I like ABBA, you like ABBA, everyone likes ABBA, but no-one in their right-mind would think that it's a good idea to record their iconic pop classic *Waterloo*, right? Wrong. We were instructed by Steve Tannett that we were going to release a version of ABBA's (Eurovision Song Contest winning) debut single, in time for the Christmas single market. We'd learnt to play it some months previously (for a laugh), but we never intended to record it. Wendi was told, in no uncertain terms, that if she refused to appear on Wogan or any-other television programme the band would be dropped from the label.

Craig Leon was to produce again and, to our delight, Roy Wood (the green-bearded glam-rock genius from Wizard and sixties psych legends The Move) agreed to play saxophone. It was another cover version, we were not at all happy (especially Wendi), but if it meant getting back on TOTP, we'd do it.

The recording session (again in Britannia Row) was great fun. Roy Wood was a delight, a fabulous and highly entertaining British eccentric with a thick 'Brummie' accent. We got on famously and enjoyed listening to his anecdotes. I was slightly surprised when he first arrived and embarrassed myself with a stupid remark that I regretted instantly...

'Hello, aren't you small!'
He didn't take offence and simply replied, 'Yes, I am.'

The video, a two-day shoot in an abandoned London theatre, was a send-up of Abba's famous appearance on the Eurovision Song Contest. A replica stage set was built to suit. Introduced in French as well as English by British thespian Katie Boil, the Anadin Brothers, dressed in the same costumes as the girls from Abba, mimicked the original dance routine, which was filmed from the same angles. The Medics, plus Roy Wood, then invaded the stage with much pomp, bursting through polystyrene walls and swinging from ropes; we took over the performance from there on.

The Euro-judges, filmed in advance, were played by Captain Sensible (larger than life guitarist from The Damned), Lemmy (blood-transfused uber-bassist from Motörhead) and our A&R man, Steve Tannet, dressed as Napoleon.

Despite good radio-play and book-makers giving 'even odds' on Waterloo becoming the Christmas No. 1, the record achieved an eventual UK chart position of number forty-five.

47. Venice

Nick Kamen was famous in the eighties for taking off his jeans in Levis adverts - and then he got a record deal. He had a band built around him, which mimed along to his hit single, often at the same Italian play-back festivals at which we were booked to do the same. At one such event, in Venice, every band (there were around ten or so) had to share a makeshift dressing room in a vacant function-room of a hotel, overlooking a temporary stage erected in the middle of an ornate Venetian town square full of enthusiastic Italians.

Most bands arrived in the clothes that they wore on stage, but we had to strip and change into our ridiculous stage costumes in front of a room full of amused show-biz types, copping a look as we undressed, pointing, staring and gawping; it was very embarrassing, spandex leaves nothing to the imagination.

As we changed, the drummer from the Nick Kamen band wandered up and struck up an awkward conversation. He introduced himself and said that he'd noticed us partying in a club in New York, The Milk Bar, a few months earlier.

'You lot were really gone,' he said, as we blushed and struggled into our clothes. 'I've never seen anyone so, out-of-it, as you lot... ever. You were fucked.'

We laughed politely and chatted back.

'Just another night on the town with the wacky Medics,' Vom joked. He didn't mention the incapacitating quantities of Chrystal Meth that had been doing the rounds.

Finally, we were ushered onto the stage for our ten-minute slot of 'being paid not to play', and then we could finally change back into normal clothes, relax and exploit the fabulous hospitality. We were treated to a floodlit tour of Venetian canals from the rear of a private boat; it looked fantastic.

'The best way to see Venice,' we were told. Everyone was in the very best of moods by the time we sat down to eat.

Patsy Kensit was famous in the eighties for eating frozen peas in a Birds Eye advert – and then she got a record deal. The child star would later go on to marry the bassist from Big Audio Dynamite, the singer from Simple Minds and the front man from Oasis, but when she was a precocious teenager she fronted her very own pop group called Eighth Wonder.

Eighth Wonder were sitting on an adjacent table from us in the posh restaurant, they'd also mimed to records in the town square. The smartly dressed band of well-groomed young session musicians gazed longingly at our table. We were in good form, buzzing with drunken laughter and the happy flirtations of the weird and wonderful. Patsy chatted louder in an attempt to hold their attention, their eyes glazed with boredom as the pretty mistress held court, discussing shoes, sunglasses and other fascinating accessories.

'I love you Patsy,' I called out as we boarded our return gondola, my hand clutching my heart. She seemed flattered, smiled warmly and waved.

'He's got VD,' Mr Vom shouted, helpfully.

Needless to say, Patsy Kensit did not marry the bassist from Doctor and the Medics.

48. Superstore

Andrew King phoned one evening with some important news.

'Richard, dear boy, Doctor and the Medics have been invited to appear on Saturday Superstore. They want the band to paint a mural, live in the studio. You being the artist of the group are the first and obvious choice to appear.'

This was a lie. Mr Vom was supposed to appear on the television show (with Clive and McGuire), but Vom's face was covered in cuts, lumps and bruises. (The result of jumping from a speeding mini-cab on a dual carriageway, escaping across a field whilst the driver radioed for backup, hiding in a ditch until he was discovered and beaten, then delivered to the local police station where the sore and sodden Mr Vom was booked for fare evasion; a fare extortionately high due to the lady stranger that shared Vom's cab, directing the driver to a miles-away destination whilst he slept; hence his attempted and ill-fated runner).

Painting the Superstore mural wasn't a problem for me, I'd done the artwork for the *Druids* single, the illustration on the back of *Happy But Twisted* and *Miracle of the Age* plus much of the Medics' fanzine *Medication*, but Mr Vom phoned to apologise anyway.

'Sorry, Dickie, I've tried covering it up with make-up, but I still look like I've been beaten up.' Which, of course, he had been.

Saturday Superstore was a popular morning children's magazine programme, presented by 'right-on' Radio 1 DJ Mike Reed and ex-'Blue Peter' girl Sarah Greene. I'd had a school boy crush on Sarah Greene for many years, which plugger Oliver Smallman delighted in telling her.

As the show opened, I sketched a life-size cartoon likeness of the band on a large purpose-built hoarding. The video of *Waterloo* was shown, and we were introduced to the television audience for a brief interview to promote the record and announce an exciting competition. Then, whilst Clive and McGuire coloured in the cartoon and I finished the mural with a thin black outline, other guests were interviewed in front of us as well. It was a lot of air time.

The finished mural was a success; it was used as part of the stage set from then onwards. I added a likeness of the presenters to the composition; Mike Reed was very pleased with his, but Sarah Greene didn't like hers at all.

'I don't look like that do I? I thought he fancied me,' she complained.

The 'exciting competition' was a stroke of genius, a groundbreaking new promotional gimmick from the mind of Oliver Smallman. The prize would be Doctor and the Medics performing the brand new single *Waterloo*, live in the competition winner's living room.

49. Bath

Everyone tried to win the Saturday Superstore 'front room gig' competition. The word spread quickly, and anticipation was high. To win, all you had to do was send in a postcard with the correct answer to a simple question - 'Who fought against Wellington at the Battle of Waterloo?' It was very easy, 'Napoleon'; everyone had a go, many had more than one. The chance to have the Medics play in your own living room was irresistible. We had visions of playing to fans of the band, avid followers since the very beginning; a trendy student who had every record or a rock music aficionado who would gain kudos amongst his peers and treasure the opportunity forever; together we would make rock history. Possibly, we allowed ourselves to dream, we might be invited to the home of a glamorous actress or supermodel and spend the day partying with the beautiful people; the lifestyle of the rich and famous. The winner turned out to be an eleven-year-old dumpling from the West Country. A young schoolgirl (who didn't have any Medics records) that watched Saturday Superstore (whose mum knew the correct answer, whose entry card was chosen at random) won the privilege of witnessing us play live in her family home; along with her younger sister, primary-school-teacher mother and un-amused father (who happened to be a policeman).

We arrived at the small terraced house on a suburban estate (on the cheap side of Bath) with our tour bus, full road crew (and stage lights), a television camera crew with their own lighting rig, plus an articulated lorry with our back-line and a hefty 5k PA system. The policeman looked on in horror as the power hungry equipment was squeezed into the tiny front room and plugged into his household electricity supply.

The camera crew filmed us dutifully miming along to *Waterloo,* but we played a twenty-minute live set for the family. The prize winner and her sister were made-up in full Anadin Brothers wigs, costumes and face-paint; the policeman stood menacingly by his electricity meter, watching the dial spin around at an alarming speed. He was very unhappy. He also didn't appreciate McGuire having a bath in his otherwise spotless tub, or me painting a mural of the band (similar to the one on the Superstore show) on his dining-room wall. He stood and grumbled as I splashed brightly coloured gloss paint over his freshly hung wallpaper.

The Policeman appeared on a later episode of Saturday Superstore, along with his precocious children (again fashioned in Anadin Brothers garb). Clive and McGuire were dragged in to sing the praises of the lovely family and invite them to attend a forthcoming Doctor and the Medics show in Bristol; they were to receive V.IP treatment.

The Bristol concert came and went, just like the policeman and his family. Clive's language was a foul-fettered stream of vulgarity and sexual content; we watched as the offended contest winners fled from their private box after the second song of the set.

50. Charity

Charity was popular in the eighties; it was good publicity and big business. Bob Geldof made it fashionable, the successes of the' Live Aid' Christmas single in 1984 and subsequent Wembley Stadium extravaganza (June 1985) surprised the entire music industry; his trademark four-letter words and scruffy enthusiasm created charity fervour, everyone wanted to get on the bandwagon. 'Live Aid' made careers; sultry jazz-pop singer Sade was unknown until her charitable performance raised awareness about starving Ethiopians.

There was an 'Indie Live Aid' concert running parallel with that of the rock stars at Wembley (at Dingwalls in Camden Lock). The Medics agreed to play. The event started around midday, the audience was required to make a charitable donation of at least £5 admission charge; lots of our fans turned up. However the bouncers kicked the audience out every few hours and made them pay another charitable donation of at least £5 for re-admission. We arrived for our evening slot, our fans had by this point made three charitable donations to see us. We were never certain that those non-voluntary charitable donations found their way into the 'Live Aid' charity chest.

After 'Live Aid' there were all sorts of charity events to help promote bands, and labels jostled to have their artists take part in these projects. Next up was 'Ferry Aid', a charity to raise money for the victims of the

Zeebrugge disaster (the capsizing of the MS Herald of Free Enterprise ferry in 1987). The Sun newspaper organised the recording of the charity hit record (the Beatles song *Let It Be)* produced by Stock Aitken and Waterman. Pop stars lined up to volunteer their services, including Doctor and the Medics.

The Anadin Brothers sang on the chorus, a camera crew filmed them for the video as they sang; Clive joked around behind them, he was politely asked not to sing. The 'everyone together' backing vocals included every member of every band (plus their respective A&R men) crooning along to the track whilst elbowing for space in the video. A photo was taken on which we could spot ourselves in the centre pages of The Sun. *Let It Be* shot straight to the top of the charts. This, we joked, was our second (minuscule involvement notwithstanding) Number One hit.

We were asked to be involved with another African relief charity, 'Sport Aid', miming along to our singles at London's QPR football stadium, packed with banner-waving school children. The after-show party was at posh Covent Garden nightclub Stringfellows.

Stringfellows was exclusive, expensive and beyond the ambitions of weirdo rock groups like Doctor and the Medics; that all changed as soon as were in the charts. We were invited to swanky parties, brimming with glamour models and TV celebrities. There was often free booze at these events, if you arrived early enough (bottles of lager, glasses of white wine or cheap champagne), but once the freebies had been exhausted, you were at the mercy of the exorbitant paying bar, and the free booze always ran out. To this end we would employ one of Mr Vom's favourite tricks, stealing people's unattended drinks - which led to another oft used Medics slang word.

Mining (n). To liberate unguarded alcohol whilst uttering the phrase 'that's mine'.

The 'Sport Aid' after-show party was empty when we arrived, so we had our choice of tables. We positioned ourselves around a large circular table, and Mr Vom and I busied ourselves at the free bar. By the time the club was full our table was covered with glasses of complimentary white wine. The free booze ran out shortly after. We guzzled the acidic plonk and watched the charitable pop personalities mingle and network. After a time, Mr Vom became decidedly shaky, eyes glazed, head wobbling with wine glasses in hand; he'd polished off three to each one that I could manage. Every time that I looked, the same two glasses were between his fingers. He seemed very furtive, and I became suspicious, but a mischievous grin was the only clue to any potentially dastardly activities. I needed the toilet and left the table. On my return Mr Vom, still seated (wine in hand) was hunched over with his hair shielding his face.
        'You alright Mr Vom?' I asked.
He looked up, smiled and put a full glass on the table. I reached for my wine, still where I'd left it.
        'Don't drink that, Dickie.'
I examined my glass; it looked ok, but I swapped it for another.
        'Don't drink that one either.'
I held the glass up to the disco lights; it seemed fine except for some tiny flecks lurking near the bottom and a faint acrid odour to the nose. I looked across our table; there were hardly any empty glasses. I'd drunk

many and Mr Vom had drained far more. As I considered the miracle of the never depleting wine, a busty woman leant across and took two full glasses. She smiled politely as she attacked our stash; her gel-headed boyfriend snatched two more.

I noticed Vom leaning over yet again, but this time I could see his mouth. He was vomiting into an empty glass. He sat up and placed the brimming glass of fresh sick on the table. I realised, as alarm rushed my senses, just what he'd done; drink one, spew one.

'How many of these glasses are puke, Vom?' I barked, observing the busty woman sip from her polluted glass and fearing for my life.

'All of them,' announced Mr Vom proudly, contemplating his work. The table was full with Mr Vom's warm vomit. The gel-headed boyfriend was sniffing his drink, lips puckered, face contorted and sour. I dragged Vom from his seat as a crowd of hapless punters raided the unguarded stash of complimentary bile. We sped towards the exit as shrieks of horror chased at our heels.

As we made our escape through Covent Garden's maze of shopping lanes, I reflected upon a time when we'd fled with a similar urgency, from an Italian beer festival; a few days of holiday time in which unsuspecting mountain folk were introduced to the bewildering proclivities of an insect-swallowing, sister-deflowering, drunken drumming nut-case. That was the last time that we were invited to the exclusive London nightclub called Stringfellows and another first for my friend Mr Vom.

51. Cocks

There are moments in time, events that on the occasion seem harmless, but, when revisited with the benefit of hindsight, must have appeared quite odd. One such innocent incident happened backstage before an otherwise uneventful gig at Brunel University. For no particular reason, Clive wanted to see my penis.

Nudity in the Medics was an everyday occurrence, what with Mr Vom's willy acrobatics and Clive's bollock-twisting practices; no-one seemed particularly phased by a naked body back-stage. However, I was very shy and always managed to preserve my modesty, I kept my pants on. My 'fight or flight' reflex ordinarily repelled me from any risky situation. However, on this occasion, I stood trapped in the corner of a full dressing room; when Clive demanded that I drop my pants (encouraged by the girls), my exit route was well and truly blocked.

I weighed up the situation, I could try to talk my way out of it, but I knew that was unlikely, everyone was calling for me to undress. I could make a sudden dash for the door, attempt to struggle my way through to the relative safety of a corridor, but there were several people to get past, and an attempted escape might escalate the situation to my further disadvantage. I had no choice; I would have to show them my tackle. What I most definitely did not want was my clothes taken from me, I might never get them back, and I could be thrown into the corridor stark naked. I needed to somehow keep control over the situation.

     'I'll show you mine... if you show me yours,' I bargained.

If somebody had walked into the dressing room during the following, carefully timed sixty seconds (the promoter, a member of staff, or a fan after an autograph) they would have been greeted with a very bizarre sight. Clive, McGuire, Mr Vom, Alex Bienkov, Martin Pyle, Harry D'mac and both Anadin brothers, lining the walls of the dressing room, arms folded and trousers down, genitals dangling in the breeze... gawping at my cock.

52. Concept

'We just want to release records,' Clive explained to an uninterested Steve Tannett; an emergency A&R meeting had been especially called at the band's request.

'No more fucking shit pop music,' Wendi added helpfully.

We'd written four new songs, none of which sounded particularly commercial (one even had an unusual time signature), but we were tired of playing the same set and needed an excuse to included a new track or two. We wanted to record a four track EP. Steve Tannett agreed, he booked us into the Zarjazz (Liquidator) Studio in Caledonian Road (owned by Two-Tone darlings Madness). Engineered by Graham Meek, who had worked on the debut album, we were to produce it ourselves.

Clive had written, so he told us at great length, four interconnected lyrics based around a singular cosmic theme, to create a narrative throughout the recording; or to use the 'prog rock' vernacular - a concept record. Throughout these four songs - *Sound Of Chains*, *Perfect World*, *Silver King* and *Age Of Gold*, the listener was introduced to a strange world in which society was championed by masters of the pinball machine. It sounded very much to us like a plot line from The Who's rock opera *Tommy*, but it was a departure from the Craig Leon produced pop fodder and something that our original fans could re-claim.

The recording went well (I designed the sleeve) and IRS released the record (through Illegal) as promised, in time for us to promote it during a hefty European tour in 1987.

Clive did his usual bout of pre-gig interviews with the press, but he found it unusually daunting. The continental journalists expected wacky sound-bites, the well-oiled banter usually spouted by The Doctor around the pop single releases, but this time they simply didn't understand what the hell he was talking about.

'It's a fully realised concept album,' he reasoned, 'except it's actually a four track EP.'

The record had the bemusing title *Two Pieces Of Cloth Carefully Stitched Together* – which had nothing to do with the concept storyline whatsoever. The running order was such that the strongest track (the most radio-friendly) was last. The weakest track was first. We only played two of the tracks live (the second and third) because they were easier to play - but neither were particularly catchy. The EP had no radio support, and the journalists couldn't follow the 'plot'. Reviewed simply on merit, comments were patchy at best. With no-one to produce the record other than ourselves, Clive's vocals, especially during the first two tracks, sounded like a deaf Elvis impersonator who had forgotten to wear his hearing aid. The record achieved a UK Indie Chart position of thirty-four.

Clive insisted on frequent plays of a cassette tape of the EP in the tour bus, immersing himself in the intricacies of his unfathomable plot. Mr Vom and I howled along in the back of the bus at the top of our voices joyfully pissed; we rolled with mischievous laughter each time one particularly badly delivered line repeated throughout the song.

'This one'z fer yu,' The Doctor crooned through the unforgiving bus speakers.

'Dickie Damage,' Mr Vom whispered, tears in his eyes and beer in hand. 'We're gonna get a slap for this.'

53. Fights

'Look what the wacky Doctor just did to me.' Mr Vom stood in the doorway, eyes swollen, face bloodied and nose broken.

Fistfights during the Medics years were fairly uncommon. Apart from Clive and Wendi punching the shit out of each other at regular intervals and Vom attacking a bar full of Italian mods, we managed to avoid violence surprisingly well. Newcastle, however, seemed (on two occasions) the exception to this rule.

The Chelsea Hotel was a 'no-star bed'n'breakfast' on the edge of town; we stayed there frequently, not just because it was cheap, but because Wendi liked the home-made lemon curd that they served at breakfast. The rooms (there were no singles) were usually cramped; multiple beds squeezed into tiny spaces that were either damp (from broken sinks that we pissed in) or a fire hazard (due to gas fires that scorched the tatty wood-chip wallpaper peeling around). It was the biggest dump in Newcastle, but they tolerated the late night comings and goings of musicians.

On one occasion, Clive, McGuire, Mr Vom and I had to share a room; whilst McGuire was busying himself in the toilet, Vom and I entertained ourselves by trampolining on the mattresses, bouncing from bed to bed in long exaggerated leaps. Inevitably one broke (the largest of the four). I landed particularly heavily and snapped one of the bed legs. Clive, finished pissing in the sink, and quickly sat on an unbroken bed; Mr Vom did the same, two beds were left. I wedged the broken leg underneath the corner of the damaged bed, it was precarious but looked ok; I then claimed the third bed and sat innocently awaiting the return of McGuire.

We cracked open a beer and chatted amiably as McGuire re-entered, he seemed genuinely touched that we'd left him the largest (presumably most comfortable) of the four beds, an unusually selfless thing to do, especially from Clive. He thanked us warmly and accepted a beer, sipping it whilst removing his grubby clothes, singing the children's bedtime song *Wee Willie Winky* and dancing a comical jig for our amusement. Encouraged by our fitful giggles, he dragged out his little skit for as long as he dared, unawares as to the real reason for our laughter. Eventually he tired, climbed into his covers, pulled them around his neck, and the bed crashed noisily to the floor.

As we smothered our laughter, McGuire tried in vain to fix his bed, busy in a flurry of contained temper and beige underpants; scratching at bent screws with his fingernails, balancing the mattress with fragments of splintered wood and beer mats. It fell to the floor loudly, repeatedly, and we couldn't prevent our hysterics. Vom jumped to his feet and assisted McGuire by handing him a beer mat. McGuire pushed Vom away.

'You bloody did this, Vom; it's always you, everything's always your fault. I'm having your bed,' he barked, grabbing Vom's shoulders and neck, twisting him under his arm into a half-Nelson lock. Vom immediately reacted to the attack with a similar move, grabbing McGuire's throat and hooking his ankles with a skilful toppling manoeuvre. Clive and I sat amused and amazed as an undersized red-haired punk grappled with a sulking yellow-haired oaf, McGuire's tatty stretched-out underpants adding to the uncanny resemblance to two drunken clowns wrestling.

Only when the body slaps turned to punches was the fight stopped; I pulled them apart, much to Clive's disappointment.

More seriously, and also in Newcastle (this time with a proper hotel), a few of us were having a nightcap after a post-gig party at a nightclub (The Mayfair). There was a knock at the door; unsteady on his feet and trembling, it was Mr Vom. With eyes puffy and sore, and crusted crimson flaking around his nostrils, he pointed at his ruined face. We were shocked; he entered and explained. Clive had picked a fight with Vom at a taxi rank outside the club. Despite being half the size of Clive, Vom braved his punches but was getting badly beaten. To even this height disadvantage, Vom tripped Clive to the floor, straddled his shoulders and landed some punches. Clive immediately submitted, insisting that his glasses were broken. Vom stopped fighting, but Clive didn't; he jumped to his feet, straightened his specs and broke Mr Vom's nose.

'Clive fights dirty.' Vom said.

54. Knickers

The Doctor and the Medics merchandising range was popular and prolific. The first Medics t-shirts were hand produced for fans and friends; car paint sprayed through scalpel-cut cardboard stencils. Denim jackets and motorbike leathers also utilised these stencilled designs to great effect.

Then came the badges, the first were hand drawn attempts (felt-tip pen and Sellotape), but a friend who worked for a printer (Cabbage Patch Chris) offered to make some real ones. We prepared a neat Medics face logo (in black) expecting small one inch button badges in return. When the manufactured badges were delivered, we received one hundred, oversized, three-inch white lapel badges; the under-scale design lost in a vast nineteen seventies chest plate. They looked ridiculously trashy, and people loved them. We eventually managed to make small button badges, which were popular with the more self-conscious types, but the die-hard fans often wore the big tacky badges with pride; the mark of a fan without shame or fashion sense.

Our first properly printed t-shirt (various psychedelic designs, versions of the Medics face and Anadin Brothers logos) were usually printed in dark Gothic colours; purples, mustards and crimsons on black. Popular with punks and flower children, but the colour palette and hallucinogenic imagery could hurt sensitive eyes. We had some simple white-on-black Medics face shirts produced, to help preserve people's eyesight (easier to focus on - if you weren't tripping), plus some limited-edition purple on white, which were nice. But, without doubt, the best item from the Doctor and the Medics merchandising portfolio was the sensationally rude 'Medics knickers'.

Fashioned from sheer black nylon with laced frills and trimming, the 'baby-doll' knickers were decorated with a white screen-printed Medics face down the tiny pubic triangle. With a long red tongue lashing underneath the gusset; they looked filthy. The Anadin Brothers each sported a pair, with micro mini-skirt, on Top Of The Pops; the camera man delighting in three minutes of up-skirt close-ups; the Medics face grinning from between their thighs, it's tongue licking to the beat of their leg's-akimbo dance routine.

After a particularly sweaty performance at a show in Milton Keynes Town Hall, Clive suggested that we all do the encore in Medics knickers – just Medics knickers. I wasn't at all sure about this, but Mr Vom had already stripped and was pulling off his wet under-crackers with one hand, the other pulling on fresh Medics knickers. McGuire agreed also.

'Nobody's gonna see anything anyway,' he said, 'the guitars will cover everything up.'

'Come on, Dickie, get them off,' Clive insisted.

'Off, off, off,' Colette chimed in, 'you start playing and we'll follow you.'

'It'll take us a while to change,' Wendi reasoned, 'our costumes take longer to remove.'
Clive had a pair of knickers in hand and was wrestling with one of his boots.

'We'll all be up there with you - with knickers on,' he promised adamantly. 'Get out there, before they stop applauding.'

Begrudgingly, I quickly stripped into a tiny pair of girl's knickers and followed McGuire and Vom on stage.

The crowd went crazy. Mr Vom disappeared behind a wall of cymbals and tom toms and started beating the kick drum. McGuire strapped his guitar over his stomach and began chugging the introduction to *Silver Machine*, his crutch hidden behind a paisley Fender Telecaster. I picked up my bass and plonked away on the strings. To my horror I realised that my guitar strap was too long for the contours of my bass to cover the knickers or my tackle. I blushed and looked at the grinning faces and pointing fingers. The girls climbed up onto the stage, fully clothed. Clive quickly followed – fully clothed and laughing.

As Colette chased me round the stage, trying to smack my buttocks and grab my exposed bollocks, Clive finished the encore; he'd got me again with another of his 'jokes'. Like some kind of Freudian nightmare - I was virtually naked, in a confined space with a thousand people staring at me, wearing nothing but ladies see-through underwear.

55. Wales

Andrew King had a small picturesque cottage on the edge of the Black Hills in Wales. Clive and Wendi had visited this cute country dwelling and loved it; they were determined to buy a similar cottage and move to Wales. To do this they planned to house hunt whilst holidaying at Andrew King's cottage; the days to be spent viewing property, evenings spent huddled around a log fire, chugging mead and eating soda bread. However, the schedule was such that the band needed to finish writing the second album. The bulk of the music was already penned by McGuire and myself (demoed on a Portastudio cassette machine ready for Clive to add his vocals). Rehearsal time was booked for the whole band to knock these songs into final shape before the album recording session, also scheduled and pre-booked. Clive just needed to finish his parts – he had two weeks.

To my annoyance, I found myself sitting in McGuire's VW camper van, driving down to Wales on my precious free fortnight, instead of going on a summer holiday as planned with my girlfriend. Clive had contrived for IRS to hire Andrew King's cottage as a 'perfect remote venue, conducive to writing the difficult second album.' I was told I'd be there for a weekend; we were there for two wet weeks.

Our long dull days were spent thusly:

Wendi would scrub the flagstone kitchen floor and cooking range, whilst we gathered fire wood and built the fire; then breakfast.

Clive and Wendi would drive out to meet an estate agent, whilst McGuire and I re-recorded the demos that we'd already written on a fresh Portastudio tape; then lunch on Clive and Wendi's return.

After lunch, we'd play what we'd re-recorded to Clive and Wendi, who had already heard the previous versions (which were exactly the same); they'd then drive to another property on their estate agent's list. McGuire and I then re-recorded yet another song that we'd already written and recorded; then dinner on Clive and Wendi's return.

After dinner, we'd play what we'd re-recorded to Clive and Wendi, who had already heard the previous versions (which were exactly the same); we'd then get drunk; then to bed.

There were two exceptions to this pointless monotony:

Andrew King told us that the record time for running from the cottage door to the highest point of an overlooking hill and back was 45 minutes. Such was my boredom that I attempted to equal this time (charging up and down the precarious rocky paths in my Monkey Boots) and on one occasion I actually beat it. As I slumped exhausted, soaked in sweat, limbs twitching from excess adrenalin, Clive phoned Andrew to proclaim my new record time. Andrew admitted that there wasn't a record time, 45 minutes or otherwise – he'd lied.

On the evening before we were finally due to return home, we visited and were 'locked-in' a local pub. I sampled a pint of every 'proper Welsh' real ale that they sold and a few of the landlord's special supply; some that tasted like roasted hops and honey and some that smelt stale, like fermented feet. My last memory of the pub was of my head thrust deep into a filthy urinal, vomiting.

As we drove home to London, I reflected upon the utter waste of time spent in that cottage (we'd written no new material, Clive had written no lyrics, and he and Wendi had not found a property); I leant from my seat and evacuated my stomach through McGuire's VW Camper Van window – it tasted like roasted hops and honey and smelt stale, like fermented feet.

56. Hippos

Despite the vagaries of the 'concept' four-track EP debacle, *Two Pieces of Cloth Carefully Stitched Together* was sonically more satisfying than much of the debut album, and as such we wanted to produce our second album ourselves. IRS agreed but on condition that we demo the entire album first; to make sure that it didn't turn out a complete mess. Recorded at Terminal Studios in the Elephant And Castle, with the promising young engineer Harvey Birrell at the controls, as with the demo recordings for the first album, the demos sounded great; tight solid rock songs with a fluid, funky rhythm section (a cross between Led Zeppelin, Sly and the Family Stone and AC/DC). They were perfect. Everyone was pleased, and IRS gave us the permission to produce the album.

Logic would suggest that as the album 'demo' recordings were 'perfect', we should, albeit with a few tweaks, release them as the album proper, but no. We were again booked into Terminal Studios, again with Harvey Birrell, whereupon we started (from scratch) to re-record each track in turn for a second time - but at a faster tempo. We then added a string section, a horn section, Hammond organ, sax solos (by Davey Payne of The Blockheads), the Anadin Brothers' 'wall of sound' backing arrangements, Clive's unusual vocal talents and layer upon layer of guitar over-dubs. It was a complete mess.

Despite the excessive tracking, Harvey Birrell was managing to come up with interesting and quite frankly brilliant, stripped-down monitor mixes. We were all confident that, with prudent muting of unnecessary or pointless parts, the album would 'come together in the mix'. However, Steve Tannett thought Harvey was too inexperienced to mix the album so booked a week at Camden's Roundhouse Studios, with Graham Meek behind the mixing desk.

Graham was an 'old school' engineer. His work on the debut album and 'concept' EP was not creative; he recorded parts cleanly and mixed them properly. Whereas Harvey Birrell understood the 'big fat' sound that we sought, unafraid to strip the track right back to basics to create space and let the songs breathe, Graham muted nothing. Each and every part was included in the mix, the string section, horn section, Hammond organ, sax solos (by Davey Payne of The Blockheads), the Anadin Brothers' 'wall of sound' backing arrangements, Clive's unusual vocal talents, and layer upon layer of guitar over-dubs; all were positioned in the mix and all sounded small, thin and cluttered.

The finished album was called *I Keep Thinking It's Tuesday*; a nod back to the Alice In Wonderland movie oft played at the Scala film festivals. The title was originally 'borrowed' from a famous surrealist cartoon in Punch Magazine from 1937 by Paul Crum involving two hippopotamuses relaxing in a watering hole, one hippo says to the other...

'I keep thinking it's Tuesday.'

The album featured such songs as *I Wanna Choke On Your Love*, *The Madman Of Bernarae* and *Take My Gorilla For Free*. It hit the shelves in 1987 and immediately received a plethora of savage reviews. Not only were there far too many parts struggling for space within the track (because we re-recorded at a faster tempo), several of the original bass parts simply didn't work - too busy and without the all important 'groove' around which many of the songs were written. Clive's vocals, once again, suffered from not having a proper producer. One review in Melody Maker was nothing but a list of everything that the journalist hated about the record – it was a long list.

Before the album was released, a single was chosen, simply called *More.*

57. Rage

Jeff the Rage was a lolloping great bear of a man with a toothy grin and mullet haircut. Recommended as 'reliable crew' for a short jaunt through Holland, his roadie nickname was actually Chewbacca (due to his resemblance to the Star Wars character), but we established our own term of endearment for him after just a few hours of our first meeting.

As we left London on the drive down to our ferry departure, Jeff asked Mr Vom if he'd remembered his passport, tour bus chatter to befriend his new employers. Vom checked his jacket pockets; he did indeed have his passport. Jeff searched his jacket pockets, too, and his shirt, jeans and overcoat pockets, plus the compartments of his tool case and luggage; he'd forgotten his passport. We watched with bewilderment as Jeff leapt from the moving bus and disappeared into a tube station.

'See you at Dover,' he shouted over his shoulder.

We didn't expect to see him again. Clive joked that 30 minutes was a record for the shortest serving Medics roadie. We braced ourselves for a tour setting up heavy stage equipment and tuning our own guitars.

To our utter surprise Jeff was waiting for us at the port, standing at the side of the road, passport in hand. He'd made a huge effort to meet us in time; we changed our opinion of the man, from blundering oaf to conquering hero within seconds of him clambering back onboard the tour bus.

Once onboard the ferry, a few of us headed for the café to line our stomachs with greasy food and arranged to meet the others in the bar afterwards. On our return we found Jeff and Harry D'mac relaxed around a table with a bottle of duty free Johnny Walker Red Label Whisky; it was half empty. Harry motioned towards Jeff; he'd consumed most of it. He was the only person I'd ever seen that drunk, that early in the morning. Jeff raised his arm straight, muscled flexed and fist clenched, a salute of boozy solidarity.

'Rage,' he announced.

'Rage?' We were confused by his breakfast inebriation.

'Rage... hard.' Jeff confirmed.

He was Jeff the Rage from that moment on – and he liked to rock.

In Amsterdam, having sampled a particularly potent space cake, Mr Vom, McGuire and I thought we heard an extraterrestrial communication reverberating through the shadowy lanes in the early hours of the morning. We looked up to the stars and noticed a double mattress thrust from a third floor hotel window. A voice howled through the shattered glass, echoing between the gabled façades.

'RAGE!'

58. More

The first single, and stand-out track, to be taken from the second album *I Keep Thinking It's Tuesday*, was a funky number with heavy riffs and big horns called *More*; it was memorable, melodic and, most importantly, it wasn't a cover version. Written and arranged with simple, catchy and repetitive parts (less is more), in our opinion it was the best thing we'd done to date; we were very excited. IRS liked it also and suggested a remix to best maximise its chart potential. They commissioned the up-and-coming re-mixer William Orbit (later to produce Madonna) to give it some pop gloss.

The video was put in the capable hands of the man that had directed the *Waterloo* video, Brad Langford; he too was up-and-coming, and we liked him. The video itself was shot as a spoof cinema trailer for a movie called *More*. We each portrayed a character; McGuire was a spiv, the girls his molls, Clive an evil villain. I was a skateboarding punk and Mr Vom played himself.

This was finally a record that we were proud of, that we were keen to promote, that was true to our roots. Released in 1987, in time for a Finsbury Park circus tent concert with The Damned, this guitar-heavy song was far more popular with what was left of our original audience; it had bollocks, and we played our revamped set with renewed vigour. However, the single received little radio play, and with just one television appearance to promote it (Melt Down) it failed to chart.

More, it appeared, was less.

59. Airports

Airports were always a hurdle; rarely did we clear customs without incident. Clive and Wendi were always looked upon with suspicion; long-haired drug-addled hippies ripe for close inspection. Clive usually handled it well, patiently waiting whilst customs officers wasted their time searching his dank luggage. Wendi carried the girl's stage make-up in a large metal tool case; her contempt towards customs officials was never left unapparent, as they spilt industrial-size containers of face powder across the counter and probed pots of messy grease paint; rolling her eyes as they complained about the stubborn residue that required make-up solvent to remove from their fingers and uniform.

McGuire, Colette and I would normally clear customs without problem but Vom attracted all sorts of interest. His passport would be checked and re-checked, his bags investigated, body frisked, clothes inspected; armed customs officers gathered to double-check their colleagues work, lest they weren't completely thorough.

There was an exception to this routine, and one that defies logic. On one occasion, I purchased a toy motor-racing helmet from an airport gift shop for Mr Vom; it matched his hair. He could just about squeeze the red plastic helmet over his head, resplendent with go-faster decals and a green retractable visor. As he approached passport control, chin-strap fastened and visor down, our roadie Josh slowly raised the visor from Vom's eyes, whilst making a gentle buzzing sound through his teeth. They were waved straight through unchecked. Amazed, they tried the same thing at customs, visor lowered covering Mr Vom's eyes, Josh buzzed the visor into the upright position, and again they were both waved through without being searched, frisked or hassled in any way.

There are two possible explanations to this riddle; either the airport officials thought that Vom was a child or 'simple' in some way, or, as I prefer to remember it, the helmet made Mr Vom invisible!

The magical properties of the toy helmet would have come in very useful with one particularly irritated customs official, on our arrival into London one evening. He spotted Mr Vom in baggage control and called us over for special attention. He left Vom's suitcase until last. Underneath the clumps of sweat-matted stage clothes and clammy underwear was a small silver chain and locket pendant. The officer, delighted with his potentially incriminating find, carefully opened the locket, cupping it in the palm of his hand to catch any illegal substances that might spill from the compartment; he looked inside, growled and threw the necklace into the suitcase in disgust.

'Get out of my sight,' he hissed.

Inside the locket was a small photograph, carefully cut from a pornographic magazine - a close-up colour picture of a woman's genitals.

60. Burning Love

During the later stages of the second album recording session, we received some exciting news. A Hollywood movie producer, who had just finished a comedy feature film about the Salem witch trials called *Burnin' Love,* liked our version of *Spirit In The Sky;* the good news was that he wanted us to record a song for the movie (which would be released as a single in the US, using edits from the feature film in the video). The bad news was that it was another cover version, the Elvis Presley number *Burning Love.*

Written by Dennis Linde and originally recorded by soul artist Arthur Alexander, the tune became famous when Elvis recorded it in 1972. With the cheesy lyric 'I'm a hunk-a-hunk of burning love,' Elvis apparently hated the song. Craig Leon was hired to produce our version.

The finished track sounded less like Doctor and the Medics than anything previously imaginable. All of the instrumentation was programmed on a synthesiser by Craig Leon, only Clive and the girls performed on it. The girls wailed a few improvised bits at the end and Clive did another Dave Vanian meets Elvis Presley impersonation over the lot.

Brad Langford made the video, he was provided with various clips from the feature film, from which he skilfully edited his own shots to create the illusion of the band being in the movie cast. Shot at Highgate Crematory, Clive wore an Elvis 'Las Vegas period' rhinestone bejewelled jumpsuit with his hair teased, pinned and back-combed into a rocker's 'D.A' with a huge lacquered quiff. We were dressed far less conspicuously (as soldiers, pilgrims or Salem towns-folk); filmed being chased through wooded paths and around tombs, eventually caught, tried for witchcraft then burnt at the stake.

The video was quite funny and made us consider our version of the song a little more kindly. That was until we saw a copy of the record. We were led to believe that the b-side of the single would be one of our own original compositions, *Stare Crazy* (a condition of our original agreement in covering the song). We would have earned some manufacturing royalties from doing this, to soothe the embarrassment of our involvement with yet another cover version. The 'dodgy covers band' image was one that we were desperate to lose. However, to our horror, IRS had put *Waterloo* on the B-side.

61. Veg

Andy Veg was the least rock'n'roll of all of our road crew; he never swore. A clean-cut, short-haired, strait-laced gentleman that wore grey suits and bi-focal spectacles, who worked for a company that brokered ships and took extended leave especially to go on a UK tour, to sell t-shirts and Medics knickers. He followed us up and down the country in his beige VW estate with a home-made merchandising stall in the back. He had his own groupie who we called Veg's groupie.

I have to thank Andy Veg for helping me on two occasions, both times at his home in Lewisham, and both times whilst I was choking on my own vomit.

Veg shared a house with his sister Fiona (see chapter 2) and brother Charley; they called it Marble Mansions (Charley was in a new-psychedelic band with Alex Bienkov and Ian 'Neds' Netherwood, called The Marble Staircase). The first event was during an evening involving several hundred psilocybin mushrooms and a bottle of whiskey; I had consumed large quantities of both and had slipped into unconsciousness. Everyone else continued to party, assuming that I'd fallen asleep, but Andy Veg noticed that I was frothing at the mouth. He and Alex Bienkov dragged me to an upstairs bathroom and held me over the bath until I'd emptied my stomach of magic mushrooms and Johnny Walker. I kept repeating the same phrase, over and over...

'Too much orange.'

The second time was after a recording session; I drank a bottle of brandy and passed out. Again I began choking on puke and again Veg and Bienkov held me over the bath until I'd thrown up the booze, but not before Clive and Mr Vom had stripped me naked and penned defamatory slogans across my body with a permanent marker pen - and had (allegedly) tried to sexually assault me with the empty brandy bottle.

62. Cucumber

We were used to playing big gigs. The Reading Rock
Festival in 1986, one act down from headliners Killing
Joke, was for us a breeze. It rained heavily as soon as
we came off stage; much of Killing Joke's audience
ran for shelter. It felt like our gig - the day was ours.
The Mission were also on the bill earlier that day, the
first time that our paths had crossed since 'the fight' in
Italy. Mr Vom nodded a polite hello to Craig, the man
he'd unceremoniously punched.
We listened to Killing Joke from the backstage beer
tent and watched Andy Veg's drunken groupie trying
to pick a fight with Wayne Hussey.

In June of '86 we were booked to play an open-air
extravaganza at the Milton Keynes Bowl, a sixty-five
thousand capacity 'festival' in a disused clay pit,
headlined by Simple Minds. The crowd included some
of the most obnoxious crew of music-hating hooligans
ever to spend £12.50 on a ticket; drunk, abusive,
chucking improvised missiles at the bands. Mick Jones
of Big Audio Dynamite (ex-The Clash) was knocked
over by a Perrier bottle filled with gravel; the punk
legend toppled as his legs buckled from the force of
the projectile smashing into his knee. Susanna Hoffs of
The Bangles was reduced to tears from the perpetual
torrent of piss-filled beer glasses and plastic cutlery.
Mr Vom made the newspaper gossip columns after he
was hit on the hand by a cucumber wrapped in silver
cooking foil.

We were bemused by the disrespectful audience, totally unlike the crowd of music lovers that usually frequent open-air concerts and 'normal' music festivals. We were used to acid popping, cider swilling, happy people, loved up on the hippie atmosphere and hash cakes. It turned out that all of the flower children were at Glastonbury; the Milton Keynes concert coincided with the Glastonbury Festival weekend. Even more annoying was that we'd been offered a slot high on the Other Stage at Glastonbury, but our management had turned it down in favour of the Milton Keynes gig, the latter paid more money.

We would never be invited to play the Other Stage at Glastonbury again, or The Pyramid Stage, or any other stage with 'a name'. However, two years later we were delighted to be booked again for the famous Glasto festival, but details were murky. On our arrival we were directed to a small area somewhere at the back of a distant field. Our third appearance at Glastonbury was in a humble marquee, one in which no other bands were playing, it was a theatre tent.

We found somebody that claimed to be in charge, who gave us a stage time long after the other stages had stopped for the night. We were not listed as playing on any line-up poster, programme or advert; nobody knew that we were there. Mr Vom, McGuire and I sat in a field with a hand-drawn sign, an arrow pointing to the tent and some badly written felt-tip words 'Doctor and the Medics - secret gig - tonight - stage time... late.' It reminded me of the time, years before, when we'd ventured off into the night to watch The Invisible Band perform at The Stonehenge Festival on the strength of a similar dubious cardboard sign.

To our amazement, the tent was packed, and the people went wild; singing their hearts out to all of our songs and throwing pre-rolled joints onto the stage.

Thrice we played Glastonbury and the third time, incredibly, was probably the best.

63. Wedding

Clive and Wendi bought a cottage in The Brecon Beacons in Wales and decided to get married; we were all invited. We drove down the night before in McGuire's VW van and hit the local pub; Clive's stag night had been in the same venue a few days previously with some locals and his best man Martin Pyle (they didn't want a hangover), but Mr Vom and myself were determined to sample as much fine Welsh fare as possible and drank ourselves senseless.

Back at our tiny bed and breakfast accommodation we entertained ourselves further with a six pack of Red Stripe lager and a game of extreme mattress trampolining. Ever since our 'trampolining' endeavours in The Chelsea Hotel in Newcastle (the broken bed incident), we had developed the activity into something of an art form. My favourite manoeuvre was to somersault from the bed against a wall; the aim being to hang, momentarily, upside down, with one's back slammed against the wallpaper, in as sculptural a position as possible, before collapsing back onto the mattress; it really hurt, but if you got it right it could look quite stylish. It made a dreadful racket though; the loud thumps on the neighbouring walls reverberated through the corridors.

We could hear familiar voices from an adjacent room and concluded that our friendly video director, Brad Langford, also a guest at the wedding, was conveniently in the room next door to ours. We banged and bashed on Brad's wall, drumming and kicking his door, shaking it on its hinges and rattling the door handle, demanding that he open up and join our revelry; thundering against the thin plasterboard walls with all of our energies until we were completely exhausted. The familiar voices stopped within the adjacent room, it fell deathly still apart from some faint whimpering.

We met Brad at the church the next day; he'd just arrived from London that morning.
We sat at the back of the church, still pissed and giggling between ourselves like naughty school kids. The organist played the wedding march, and the bridal party glided up the aisle towards the groom. Colette was the bridesmaid, she looked gorgeous, her dress matched Wendi's, who also beamed. The Victorian reproduction costumes were decorated with delicate lace, mother-of-pearl buttons, cream satins and antiquated vanilla silks; Wendi's own creation, they both looked really good. Colette's boyfriend, at the time, was a bronzed, raven-haired, public school hippie named 'Handsome Richard', Wendi asked him to design and tailor Clive's wedding suit. From our

position we could see Clive's head and shoulders, but not what he was wearing. We expected him to be sporting a flashy bespoke suit befitting his assumed pop star persona; a copy of Mick Jagger's wide-lapelled three-piece flared linen number in which he married Bianca, or a slim-cut, double-breasted favoured by George Harrison when he married Patti Boyd; we waited in polite anticipation to see Clive's special threads.

To help pass the time during the inevitable monotony of the service, I carefully folded and shaped my wedding programme into long triangular points, and with two small tears in the cardboard I managed to fasten the improvised moustache to my nostrils. Mr Vom found this highly amusing and insisted that I make an origami facial ornament for him too.

The ceremony was nice and eventually the organist hammered out the celebratory chords as the happy bride and groom walked towards the exit hand in hand. This was to be the first time that Clive would see us that day, still drunk with large flapping things dangling from our noses; he glared at us, affronted by our disrespectful tomfoolery. We watched the procession nonchalantly, poker-faced, trying not to laugh – until we saw his suit. Handsome Richard (a fashion school drop-out) had made what resembled an ensemble of saggy cloth sacks. Instead of the figure-flattering sleek-lined outfit that we'd expected, Clive was 'wearing' a shapeless baggy grey bag. It hung around his tall skinny frame like a fat man who had lost seven stones in weight, crumpled, loose and hilarious. We burst into fits of laughter. We were asked to remove our moustaches soon after.

The reception was in a scenic country pub; it had three rooms. One for the marvellous buffet spread, another for the guests to sit and enjoy their dinner and drink toasts to the bride and groom - and an out-of-the-way back room for the musicians. Mr Vom, McGuire, Roman Jug and myself were told to sit in the snug bar whilst all the other guest sipped champagne and made long speeches; only when they had helped themselves to the buffet were we allowed to touch the food, by that point we were paralytic. Mr Vom threw up repeatedly (the better to utilise the free bar). Roman kept complaining of heart palpitations, the result of too much whiskey. I was reprimanded by Clive's father, who took a dislike to my skin-tight silver mohair suit and my suggestive dancing with Clive's mother.

We were the last ones to leave at closing time, a half-eaten honey glazed ham surreptitiously smuggled back to our room.

      'There appears to be a suspicious piece of ham in my bed,' McGuire surmised whilst Mr Vom bounced against the walls.

64. Way down

Everyone was deflated by the disappointing sales of *More*; however another single was selected from the second album, a catchy yet lyrically confusing ditty about piloting an airplane, called *Drive He Said*. Once again William Orbit was hired to smooth out the rough edges. McGuire and I were invited to the studio session to sit in on the remix, but William Orbit didn't like musicians in the studio with him.

'The humidity generated from people's body heat can cause the machines to become temperamental, the tape-heads to misalign and the iron oxide on the quarter-inch tape to fail,' he explained in all nonsensical seriousness.

IRS didn't want to pay for another video or expensive pluggers; released in 1988 *Drive He Said* failed to chart; this despite putting a popular live track on the B-side.

Ride The Beetle was a song about a VW Beetle motorcar, during which the audience were invited to lay on their backs and wave limbs in the air like dying insects. A song usually left for the encore, on one occasion Mr Vom felt faint from the heat of the stage lighting and needed five minutes to catch his breath. I put down my bass and climbed behind the kit to perform a shambolic interpretation of *Ride The Beetle.* I flailed away at the drums whilst the crowd rolled around spoiling their clothes on the wet, slimy floor. It went fairly well until the first drum roll when I lost the beat completely, where upon the rhythm section reduced to an approximation of smashing dinner plates and cardboard boxes falling down stairs. The audience didn't seem to notice, and the venue's soundman (a polite chap with a bad student haircut and national health specs named Justin) said that he couldn't tell the difference, but Vom was back on stage, sharpish.

Once it had become painfully apparent that *Drive He Said* had flopped entirely, morale within the band reached an all time low. Andrew King called an emergency meeting; he had news.

'It's all fucking IRS's fault, no video, no proper plugging,' he moaned. 'But there is a silver lining,' he announced optimistically. 'The second term is about to run out, IRS have one week to pick up the next album option, if they don't - we are free to move to another label.'

Record contracts often have a clause called an 'option period'; typically there would be two option periods. The label signs a band to record an album, if the album does well the label has an option (the first option) to continue the terms of the deal by paying another advance for a second album. If the second album does well the label has another option (second option) to continue the terms of the deal in a similar manner. There is typically a six week period (option period) in which the label can make this decision. IRS had not mentioned a third album and time was almost up.

'There are two possibilities,' Andrew continued, 'either IRS have simply forgotten when the term ends, which happens from time to time, or they plan to drop the band. If we remind them, and they pick up the option, they'll have to pay us another small advance, and we have to record another album, which they will, no doubt, fuck up. If they've forgotten, or if they drop the band, we will be free to sign another record deal with a bigger and better record label, with a substantially larger advance.'

It is a truism, yet one that is hard to admit (especially if you are in a group that has had some success), that the lifespan of a band is often limited and finite. Our conceit was such that we did not recognise that we had simply run our course. Our second album was the death-rattle of the band, and IRS didn't want to pay for our funeral; they were about to drop us, and we would most likely split up. Andrew King knew this, but also knew that 'the way down' can generate as much money as 'the way up', he wanted to keep us together and working for as long as possible.

'I suggest that we keep quiet,' Andrew confided, his voice serious and conspiratorial, 'and hope that IRS forget to pick up the option.'

We discussed our future; IRS were the reason for our reputation as a one-hit wonder covers band, for the embarrassment of *Waterloo* and *Burning Love.* For the failure of our self-produced second album and the single *More* that should by rights have been a hit. We would not mention a third album in the hope that we could leave IRS and sign to another label; we needed a fresh start. With refreshed confidence and a steely new purpose, we would record new demos and prepare our further carer.

'Doctor and the Medics are a fucking number one act,' Andrew roared, stoking our newly fuelled determination and straightening his tie to show that he meant business. 'We will be able to walk into any major record label and sign a brand spanking new record deal with anyone we fucking well choose. They'll be lining up to sign us.'

Andrew King

65. Scotland 1

Despite Andrew King's assurances, no other record labels were interested in signing Doctor and the Medics after IRS dropped us, major, indie or otherwise. A hurried batch of new demo recordings (including yet another cover version, *Run Run Run* by Jo Jo Gunne) tempted no-one, but that didn't stop the work offers from coming in; some were very lucrative and spectacularly weird.

The 'way down' can be every bit as much fun as 'the way up' just so long as you can admit to yourself that the ride is coming to an end. Mr Vom and I were the first to realise that our days were numbered and were determined to enjoy every last moment. This was our mindset as we found ourselves on a heavily delayed flight to Scotland in the middle of a thunderstorm. As the drinks trolley crashed into the serving gantries and the panic-stricken stewardesses strapped themselves into emergency positions, swearing under their breath, Mr Vom and I sat happily pissed (already tiddly from the airport bar), making jokes and doing impressions of the pilot and his unconvincing reassurances that this was merely some mild turbulence. We landed safely enough but were very late for our stage time; the promoter was ready and waiting to speed us to the venue.

We had been offered this particular gig before, but the management didn't regard it for a second; now that we were without a record deal we turned down nothing and agreed to the bizarre request, apart from the girls, who refused to do the show. Clive, McGuire, Mr Vom and I agreed to what only a year previously would have been too demeaning an engagement to consider. The owner of a small discotheque wanted us to mime along to our records whilst the videos played on TV screens. It sounded simple, but we were very nervous, we had performed live in small clubs on tiny stages in front of Scottish crowds before, and we'd mimed before thousands of screaming Italians at Playback Festivals and on TV, but we had never mimed on a small stage to a small audience; it just seemed wrong.

The club was full, and we were ushered into a mezzanine 'VIP' area to prepare.

'You're on in ten,' the promoter insisted. We weren't anywhere near ready, we complained, we needed to change into our stage clothes and psych ourselves up to perform. The promoter cleverly suggested that we sample a favourite local tipple, the '10/80-Snakebite', a lethal blend of heavy Scottish ale and strong cider. We knocked back a couple of viciously potent pints in time to be shown onto the stage without having time to blink, think or change.

Clive flicked a switch on the battery operated karaoke microphone and introduced himself to the wall of blank faces. He then switched it off as the first of three singles crackled through the small PA system and a video appeared on monitors around the club. We jumped about and pretended to strum and drum along to *Waterloo*, Clive dutifully lip-synched his parts. Despite the girls' absence, the fact that we were obviously not playing our instruments (the guitars weren't plugged in, and there were no amps) and that Clive's voice sounded entirely different when he turned off the mic - the crowd roared with appreciation. We dutifully 'didn't play' *Burn*, and as the encore we 'didn't play' *Spirit In The Sky*; the crowd loved it.

'We don't get many successful bands around these parts,' explained the extremely happy promoter, 'this has been a real treat for everyone. It doesn't matter that you were miming.'

As we quaffed more alcohol in the VIP bar afterwards, chatting to enthusiastic punters in their best shirts and tiny black cocktail dresses, we agreed to return and do it again soon.

It had been a fun and very successful little jaunt, if a tad bizarre; the return visit however would be far, far messier.

66. Spain

Bazza Gorman (not his real name) was our tour manager for a couple of post IRS tours. The first, in Spain, resulted in Bazza throwing a flight case at me. He took umbrage to a little song that I'd written, that we'd sing in the van when drunk. Sung to the simple melody of the children's tune *I Can Sing A Rainbow*, it made Bazza Gorman quite furious; the lyrics were as follows:

> Red and fluffy and bald and mean
> Chubby and puffy and fat
> He's a' Bazza Gorman
> Bazza Gorman
> He should wear a hat

This innocent ditty became a favourite after-show sing-a-long, the result being Bazza Gorman lugging a heavy guitar flight case (including contents) at my chest when I was in bed; it cracked a rib. It was quite painful for a time, but didn't deter me from the song.

Bazza Gorman scolded Mr Vom after a show, when he (allegedly) attempted to kick an empty wine bottle up an unguarded orifice of Gordon the Caterpillar, who'd travelled to Spain especially to see us, then got drunk and passed out in the dressing room - delaying us from leaving the venue. Gordon was abandoned on the floor in a puddle of puke and left to find his own way to the hotel. Bazza was not amused.

Bazza also spoilt a very pleasant moment in which an extremely attractive Spanish girl, who spoke little English, was so eager to communicate her wish to accompany me to my hotel room that she unbuckled my belt and thrust her hand down my trousers in the middle of the busy street. Bazza rudely pushed her away and dragged me into the van; this too was, I believe, the result of his strong dislike for my continued work on the song. The second verse developed as follows:

> Round and shiny and pink and camp
> Roly and poly and fay
> He's a' Bazza Gorman
> Bazza Gorman
> It's a Bazza Gorman day

One particular Spanish venue had a very late stage time; it was well into the early hours of the morning by the time we had finished our set and returned to the beach-front hotel; a few of us decided to sit on the beach and wait for the sunrise. As Harry D'mac, Josh and Clive sat on the sand, drinking and chatting, Mr Vom and I became fascinated with a heavy fog that hung over the Mediterranean, a dense low cloud that suspended a few inches above the waves. It was the thickest sea mist that we'd seen, and we set about to investigate; wading out through the black lapping waves towards the curtain of white vapour. Fully clothed and with a beer in hand, the water was soon over our knees and creeping up past our waists; we looked back, they were waving, we waved back and continued to stride out to sea. Our destination was for the compelling six inches of clear air that magically existed between the waves and the fog, by the time that we'd got there the water was up to my shoulders. Mr Vom, who was bouncing on tip-toes, held his beer above the waves that lapped around his neck.

We looked back to the beach; we were a hundred metres out to sea and completely invisible, hidden deep in the cloak of cloud. As the sea rippled around our faces, we relaxed and listened to the watery sounds, meditating on the splashes, plops and eerie silences in the inky dark. We could hear Clive and Harry shouting somewhere in the far distance, calling our names, worried for our safety; we were quite touched by their concern. Too good an opportunity to miss, we didn't shout back, to quell their concerns of our imminent danger, fears that we may have drowned in the perilous murky waters, but bobbed our way through the waves, parallel to the beach, until their frantic shouts were barely audible; only then, some thirty minutes later, did we wade back onto the shore. Clive's silhouette was a tiny fleck in the distance, half a mile up the beach.

By the time that they noticed us in the far distance, finally walking back into earshot, it was daylight. They hurled many incoherent insults and half-formed profanities through the dawn chorus of seagulls and faraway early traffic. We slunk back up the empty beach, sporting stupid grins, our clothes sopping wet and empty beer bottles still in hand. Clive and Harry sprinted towards us, sand flicking up around their heels as they ran; not to greet us with pats and hugs, relieved at our safety and physical well-being - but to beat the shit out of the both of us.

67. Scotland 2

Stop The Joke (verb phrase). To request an official end to a practical joke that is untimely or has run its course.

As I stood in the doorway of Clive and Mr Vom's hotel room, still drunk and late for our early morning flight, wearing a pair of crushed velvet hipster trousers and nothing else, I was still convinced that my stolen clothes would be returned.

'Ok,' I said, 'stop the joke.'

The day before had started on an optimistic high; it was our second visit to the Scottish nightclub in which we had triumphantly mimed along to three songs in return for money and alcohol. The return booking, such was the success of the first performance, paid double the fee. We had been looking forward to it, as was the promoter who was expecting to make a tidy profit; the ticket price had also doubled. We agreed to lengthen our show by an extra three minutes; the club had acquired the video to *More*.

Having been booked onto an earlier than necessary flight (the promoter didn't want to risk the rush and panic of the previous engagement), the weather had been kind this time and we arrived at the venue with plenty of time to relax, chatting to the staff and enjoying the liquid hospitality. A tray of triangular sandwiches with the crust removed awaited us in a storeroom (the dressing room), which we left untouched and made straight for the glitz and glamour of the VIP bar. The club had, over the preceding months, been showing a video recording of our first appearance, to stir up excitement and ticket sales; the night was sold out weeks in advance.

'Those high kicks went down a treat last time.' The promoter pointed at a screen as he plied us with 10/80-Snake Bites. 'Be sure to do lots of high kicks again, you'll go down a storm. People have been looking forward to this night for a long time.' Anticipation was obviously high; we couldn't wait to get on stage.

'And you're going to change into your weird and wonderful theatre costumes this time, right?' We watched the video of our club debut, jumping around in our everyday clothes, Clive was camping up his performance more than usual, high-kicking wherever possible to help divert attention from the Anadin Brothers' non-appearance; the girls hadn't joined us this time either.

'Yep,' Clive assured him, 'there'll be high-kicks and tacky stage clothes a-plenty.'

It should be noted that the club promoter made a fatal error at this point, not the band; he assumed that as we were merrily drunk on the first occasion (to help soothe concerns about miming instead of playing), he should endeavour to repeat that same level of inebriation - but when we played live we very rarely became so utterly pissed that we couldn't function. The moment that Clive told the promoter about our beer drinking competitions, and he suggested that we have a couple of rounds of 10/80-Snake Bite speed drinking, it was never going to turn out well. Come stage time we were lagging, especially me, who had to race various VIP bar liggers who were up for a challenge.

'We'll do this on stage,' Clive joked.

'Ok,' agreed the promoter, 'I'll have the drinks lined up ready.'

Resplendent in our finest stage gear, to rapturous applause, we jumped, mimed and high-kicked along to our video of *Waterloo*, drunk. I was dangerously close to falling off the stage but just about kept it together as the track faded, the crowd cheered and Clive flicked on the microphone to work the audience.

'Anyone who can drink a pint of snakebite faster than our bass player will win another free pint,' he announced. Up jumped a thirsty Scotsman who was handed a pint, as was I. Clive got the crowd to count down, and we gulped down the drinks before the *Burn* video started. I felt bloated and nauseous but moved my hands in approximate time to the track.

Clive made exactly the same announcement after the second video, up jumped another boozy Scot, and I lost a second round of speed drinking. After this second defeat, I collapsed to the back of the stage and slumped onto a chrome barrier that divided the stage from a balcony seating area behind, my bass hanging around my knees. The video of *More* buzzed through the speakers and the rest of the band continued to perform without me, as I sat out the song in a state of semi-consciousness. The crowd started to heckle.

'Sober up.'

Next was *Spirit In The Sky*. On hearing the opening chords, I suddenly became reanimated and jumped to my feet with refreshed energy and vigour; at this point proceedings became chaotic. Clive took my bass from around my neck to mime the bass part. I took his microphone and started to sing the vocals. I remembered the promoter's advice to 'high-kick' and chucked my legs around the stage, shouting into the mic, a microphone that Clive had forgotten to switch off.

'SPIRIT IN THE SKYYYYY,' I bellowed as the audience watched in horror.

I chanced to look behind me; Mr Vom was killing himself with laughter, his head nodding encouragement. I took his enthusiasm as a signal to once more switch instruments. I pushed Vom from behind the hired kit; he took the microphone and swapped it with Clive for the bass. Up until this moment most of the audience had been dancing, now they all stood open-mouthed and rigid. Although relieved that I'd stopped howling into the mic, they now had to endure my drumming. I smacked the drums as hard as I could, in my mind I became John Bonham and John Bonham, as did I, played loud. Crack, crack, crack, I whacked the snare drum, crack, crack, crack, I didn't stop until the drumsticks snapped, wooden splinters flying across the stage and behind my head; and then it was over.

The audience formed an orderly queue past the box office as they left, to demand their money back. Only once the promoter had finished refunding all of the ticket money did he call the ambulance to take the girl, whose eye had been cut open by a sharp drumstick fragment, to hospital; she was later to sue the venue. In the meantime, the band sat in the VIP bar, drinking with staff and the few punters who remained, all except for me. I was frantically checking the dressing room bins, crates and cupboards for my change of clothes; they had vanished, as had my stage shirt, mysteriously 'disappeared'. I hung my bass guitar around my neck, the better to hide my topless torso and reluctantly joined the others at the bar.

The following morning I awoke in my shared hotel room with McGuire, I still couldn't find my clothes. McGuire was already dressed, he hadn't seen them. Mr Vom and Clive were also ready to leave for the airport. This was Clive's doing, I reasoned, he must have my clothes.

'Ok, stop the joke,' I demanded (the words that officially require the ending of such practical jokes as hiding clothes minutes before we need the leave for the airport). Clive denied all knowledge.

'At least give me my shirt back,' I begged. Mr Vom threw me a t-shirt from his bag and we rushed to the promoter's car; we were in serious danger of missing our flight home.

'Do you remember that girl?' Clive asked as we sped towards the airport.

'What girl?' I didn't.

'She was a pig,' added the promoter helpfully.

'No?' I really didn't.

It transpired that in an attempt to sober up, to avoid more drinking, I decided to busy myself with a local strumpet, this I did in a very public fashion. She was blonde and, according to the promoter, not very attractive.

'You are banned from my club for life,' the promoter said as we bade our farewells.

The flight home was torturous, not just because of my vicious hangover, but because the shirt that Mr Vom had kindly leant me was a tiny bright yellow vest, which did not match my blue skin-tight velvet flares or white pointed Chelsea Boots.

Martin Pyle awaited us in London, he dropped us off at McGuire's flat in Deptford, who refused to drive me home to Eltham, but did eventually condescend to take me and my heavy guitar flight case to a busy high-street cab office in Greenwich market on a Sunday afternoon, still dressed in my ridiculous stage trousers and Mr Vom's canary yellow blouse that was cropped above the navel.

My clothes were discovered, along with my shoes, keys and wallet in an industrial dustbin outside of the nightclub some weeks later.

68. Greece

'Two shows in an old open-air theatre, on one of the rowdier Greek islands; the money's not great, but there's the possibility of delaying the return flight - to stay on for a few days free holiday,' Andrew King explained, 'would you like to do it?' We said that we would, and the band, crew and entourage flew to Greece for a week of fun, sun and Metaxa.

Once our two engagements (with plush marble-clad hotel accommodation) in a generic Greek tourist town were successfully completed, we were left to our own devices and free to travel to the coastal area. The engagements went well (the yet to be mentioned 'superhero' incident notwithstanding), but it was the free holiday (our first time in Greece) that everyone was really there for.

Clive, Wendi and Harry D'mac flew home after the shows but everyone else headed straight for the beach and rented cheap holiday rooms. Our seaside posse consisted of Colette plus her boyfriend (Handsome Richard), a man who enjoyed wearing a ladies thong on the beach. Gordon the Caterpillar and a random girl that he'd invited from his local pub. TM Bazza Gorman and Josh the roadie, plus McGuire, Mr Vom and myself with girlfriend Mads. Also in attendance, for reasons which none of us could fathom, was an occasional Gossips punter surfer chick, who we named Tequila due to her boast of regularly consuming a bottle of Tequila without intoxication. When we tested this claim, she managed four shots before swearing at the evening traffic, having sex in a public car park with Josh and passing out in a puddle of seawater, sand and sick.

By day, we'd bathe on the scorching beaches and swim in the sparkling water, at night we doused ourselves with after-sun and headed for the liveliest bars along the busy main drag. The roads at night were full of young holidaymakers whizzing back and forth on 'twist and go' mopeds (which Tequila enjoyed shouting at when intoxicated). One morning Handsome Richard pulled up on a moped with Colette on the back, Josh had a bike too (a 100cc Suzuki) with Mr Vom on the pinion. I went to the beach with Mads as they fizzed off to explore the countryside. That evening, whilst I soothed my chronic sunburn with moisturiser, the riders told tales of navigating sea roads and mountain passes and of how they planned to do the same the following day, but this time faster, on powerful super-bikes I set my mind to follow them but on a Vespa or Lambretta, a sixties motor scooter befitting my preferred youth culture, the mods.

As Handsome Richard and Colette purred along the main drag on a Suzuki 750, closely followed by Josh on a 1000cc Ducati with Vom grabbing on for dear life, I wheeled the only motor scooter available from the hire store onto the busy main road. A number of issues concerned both me and Mads that morning; she was supposed to ride on the back. Firstly, I had sun stroke. Secondly, the scooter was ghastly, not the type beloved by mods but a modern grey plastic monstrosity with ugly lines and angles that resembled something from Star Wars. Thirdly, I'd never ridden a scooter before.

Josh showed me how to operate the controls and suggested that before attempting to navigate mountain passes, I follow him along the road (without Mads on the back) until I became used to the machine. I agreed and prepared myself to drive. I pulled my cotton sun-hat hard down over my ears and pressed the electric ignition. Remembering Josh's instructions, I revved the engine, released the clutch and was off, riding a motor scooter for the first time and at a steady 15 miles per hour. Josh shouted to change into second gear. I depressed the clutch, engaged second gear and, whilst maintaining engine revs, slowly released the lever. Immediately the front wheel shot from the ground and up above my head, I was doing a wheelie and accelerating towards the traffic. Car horns beeped, the engine span, people shouted, Mads screamed, and I fell off of the back as the machine flipped over backwards, crashing into pieces of plastic and metal beneath the wheels of a truck.

We pushed it back to the hire shop and ran.

We took this dangerous, scooter-destroying, hangover induced episode in our stride; it was nothing compared to the events from a few days previously, on our first evening in Greece. Our hotel was near the bottom of a steep hill with bars, clubs and restaurants at the top. Once settled into our hotel rooms and changed into our finest summer outfits, we ventured up the hill into the warm evening in search of kebabs and lager; we found both. Mads felt ill so stayed in the room; Mr Vom encouraged me to make the most of 'a free pass'.

As soon as we'd filled our stomachs with cubed lamb and pita bread and sampled two or three drinking establishments, we settled in a tourist bar come discotheque, complete with glitter ball. I sat at the bar with Mr Vom as various band and crew members came and went. We sipped domestic lagers and danced to AC/DC records on the small illuminated dance floor. As the evening progressed I found myself dancing to pretty much every record on the dance floor, Van Halen, Judas Priest and Twisted Sister. I also danced to the shitty Euro-Disco tracks that played after the obligatory rock section. I even danced to *Spirit In The Sky*, I was really very drunk indeed.

Mr Vom had stopped dancing, content to sit at the bar and chat, whilst generously ordering fresh rounds for my return. Every time I sat down there was another beer waiting. Harry D'mac joined us and insisted on buying me drinks as well. It was around this time that Vom and D'mac became complacent in their devious plans, I noticed a glass of Metaxa being quickly tipped into my fresh glass of lager. They had been lacing every glass with a shot or two of lethal Greek spirits, vodka, whiskey and anything else that they thought would hurt. I suddenly felt the alcohol destroying my brain and wobbled to and fro in a drunken panic. Vom and Harry creased with laughter, as I staggered into the town square in search of a medicinal kebab to soak up the alcohol; I needed grease.

Mr Vom decided to join me but bumped into McGuire who was mooching around the area, and they eventually returned to the bar. During this time there were unsubstantiated reports that a coffin lid may or may not have been removed from resting outside of a house doorway (a tradition for a funeral the following day) and used as an ad hoc surf board to slide down the hill to the hotel. Whether Mr Vom or McGuire were responsible I cannot confirm, but the unsubstantiated report came from Mr Vom and McGuire themselves, in discussion at breakfast with Harry D'mac the next morning, my name was not mentioned. It was, however, mentioned in regards to another matter, the episode that was to be referred to as the 'super hero' incident.

I left Vom and Harry in the bar at around 2am but didn't go to the hotel, in truth I cannot be sure where I went, but at 8am in the morning Mads was woken by a knock on the door, it was me, and I was covered head to foot in dirt and vomit. I peeled off my clothes and collapsed into bed.

'Have you been sick?' Mads asked.

'No,' I managed before passing out.

The following morning, she inspected my smelly clothes. My shirt was caked with a chalky white substance. My trousers were also completely covered in the same pale dried bile, as were the insides of my pockets, wallet, shoes and socks (inside and out), all saturated with dirty puke. My matted hair looked like an old floor cloth.

At breakfast, Mr Vom and Harry D'mac sat a table's distance away, pointing and firing filthy looks. They were expecting an apology from me, but I had no idea why. Harry finally complained of a cut to his shoulder and held up his forearm to show me a large graze running the full length. Mr Vom also was bloodied and bruised.

'You fookin' did this,' Harry complained, 'came charging down that hill and threw us over the fookin' wall into the fookin' bins.'

'It was mad.' Mr Vom sounded baffled. 'You attacked us out of nowhere, it was like you had super strength or something, just picked us both up over your head and chucked us over a big brick wall, then ran off, disappearing down the hill.'

'Growling like a mad dog and talking insane fookin' shit.'

'Dickie Damage became Dick the Barbarian,' Mr Vom muttered, nursing his wounds.

With the benefit of eye-witness accounts and some deductive reasoning, the post-disco bar events of that evening are as follows, times are approximate:

12. Midnight. Mr Vom and Dick Damage attended the disco-bar.

2am. Dick Damage left the bar to find an open kebab shop; it is uncertain as to the success of this plan.

2.15. Mr Vom left the disco-bar (Harry D'mac remained). Mr Vom met McGuire whereupon they may or may not have stolen a coffin lid. McGuire returned to the hotel, Mr Vom returned to the disco-bar.

2.30. Mr Vom and Harry D'mac left the disco-bar for the hotel.

2.40. Mr Vom and Harry D'mac heard fast running footsteps and garbled shouts.

2.41. Dick Damage transformed from his mild-mannered secret identity into his superhero alter ego (Dick the Barbarian) whereupon he sprinted down the hill and apprehended his villainous foes (Mr Vom and Harry D'mac). Once Dick the Barbarian had dealt with these heinous enemies, and justice was seen to be done, he made a swift getaway, disappearing into the dazzling glow of the Greek sunrise.

2.45. Dick the Barbarian got lost.

3.00 – 7.50. Dick the Barbarian passed out in a hotel car park and rolled around in his own vomit for several hours.

8am. Dick the Barbarian returned to his hotel room.

Dick the Barbarian's secret identity was compromised by the aforementioned events; he was, from then on, forced to retire from crime fighting.

69. Low

It was another 'stop the joke' moment; my clothes had mysteriously vanished, and I reluctantly steeled myself to the prospect of cycling home through the busy London rush hour in Nazi Jackboots, my pink crushed velvet catsuit, rubber gauntlets and a harlequin mask stuck to my face with toupee glue.

Mr Vom had wisely opted out of these latest shenanigans (his imminent departure was fast approaching), and quite frankly it was a little embarrassing. It was another brainchild of our video director Brad Langford; a TV game show, written around Doctor and the Medics called 'How Low Will You Go?'

Clive was the compère (assisted by the Anadin Brothers), he asked the questions, McGuire was 'the house orchestra' (just him on his synthesiser). I was to assume a persona, similar to that of a TV character, The Phantom Flan Flinger, from the children's television show 'Tizwas' (to chuck shit at contestants) and Mr Vom was supposed to be the scoreboard (displaying the points whilst clad only in his boxer shorts).

I was asked to storyboard the pilot, scheduled at a studio complex in London's Tower Bridge. It all looked good on paper, but Vom was conveniently busy on the day of filming. We roped in two friends to act as contestants, one of whom, Jim Moir, would do anything to help further his career (later to become famous as comedian Vic Reeves); fashioning one of his trademark mohair suits, he added to the non-gravitas of proceedings; 'How Low Will You Go?' was a comedy game show. The point of the game was to determine how much humiliation you were prepared to endure to win a car.

Once the set was prepared, and we were changed into our respective costumes, filming began. Brad was behind the lens and directing as we went. McGuire improvised a short theme-tune and the girls introduced the contestants, whilst I squirted them with a water pistol machine-gun. Clive asked contestant number one to perform a vaguely degrading task, whilst I squirted him with a water pistol machine-gun. If the contestant completed the task correctly (which actually happened) then he received 'one point', and McGuire played a congratulatory melody, whilst I squirted him with a water pistol machine-gun. Next, Clive directed a similar challenge towards contestant number two (Jim Moir), which he performed incorrectly; and then it was finally time for my part, to execute punitive measures.

'Ok, Dick Damage,' Brad commanded, 'you're on.'

Behind me were a number of large builder's tubs, each labelled as containing uniquely unpleasant contents (baby sick, frogspawn, donkey sperm) and brimming with home-made slime (flour and water, eggs, sour milk and food colouring). I put my battery-operated machine-gun back in its holster, low-slung around my waist, and carefully grasped the sides of a bucket with my pink marigold washing-up gloves. I dragged the heavy gloop across the studio floor (accompanied by a threatening melody from McGuire's keyboard), power-lifted it level to my chest and tipped the entire disgusting contents over the contestant's head. He was instantly soaked to the skin.

Filming stopped for several minutes, for the cast and crew to stop laughing, mop up the flooded soundstage and for Jim to stop whimpering and towel himself down. We finished filming as the drenched contestant sat shivering in his ruined suit, but I was banned from further interaction with the contestants.

McGuire was later to tell somebody, who enquired as to the success of our game show...

'Richard ruined it.'

When it was time to leave, I couldn't find my clothes, once again they were not where I had left them, once again stolen by Clive who was nowhere to be seen. I had cycled that morning through the London traffic to the studio on my mountain bike; having to suffer the return journey in my skin-tight crushed velvet catsuit was another of Clive's famous jokes.

'Stop the joke,' I pleaded.
I eventual found some old overalls in a workman's skip and avoided the humiliation of peddling the many miles home in my outrageous pink one-piece.

The Medics game show was never commissioned, however an almost identical format appeared on ITV a year or so later, with Radio 1 DJ Mike Smith and camp comedian Julian Clary presenting, but oddly, there was nobody dressed in a glam-rock superhero outfit drowning the set with gallons of slimy liquid.

70. Groupies

You can usually tell when a band is about to become successful, the girlfriends get better looking. The uncanny knack that aspiring groupies have for spotting a 'tip-for-the-top' is an infallible measure in the ruthless lottery that is the music business; they know who is truly 'on the way up', and likewise they know when to jump ship. They sense the best moment to abandon a band that is on the slide and move onto the next 'in vogue' rock group. Often, the less ambitious girl will simply change bands (like changing buses), switching tours with a member of the crew (roadies don't mind 'sloppy seconds'). Maybe a girl is herself in a band; another pop-star boyfriend can only help her cause, manoeuvring from musician to musician, gaining recognition as she climbs the ladder to the more famous bands; a really skilled lady may even manage to marry into the money. The more aspiring careerist groupie, one that has designs to work in the music industry, will exploit the contacts made during the relationship and successfully negotiate the leap from groupie to (usually) Press Officer. At this point they can finally stop shagging musicians.

Doctor and the Medics were never fully introduced to this groupie formula. There were exceptions, obviously (some included within in these pages), micro-relationships blazing briefly within the hotel rooms of various continents, plus random snogging bouts with miscellaneous, 'mostly' pretty females in the darkened corners of Gossips or Stringfellows, but often these opportunities were spoilt by the home team; the Anadin Brothers simply scared rival women away.

Mr Vom had various 'mini-Vomettes' that followed him around, small punky girls with matching red spiky hairstyles; one even gifted him with a washing machine and other kitchen furniture to better nest their futures together. I was stalked by a gaggle of young girls that frequently appeared at shows wearing specially screen-printed psychedelically designed 'Richard Searle Fan Club' t-shirts, resplendent with a cartoon picture of my face and swirly lettering. They chanted suggestive slogans and handed me perfumed letters describing their adolescent desires in lurid Biro'd detail. Despite this flattering, if worrying, attention (plus a free t-shirt), they never achieved groupie status; that is to say, never with me – one by one, McGuire went through the lot.

71. Norman

The ubiquitous, general knowledge board game, rife across coffee tables in the mid-eighties, *Trivial Pursuits*, introduced a number of alternative question boxes, including a set on sport (orange box) and another on music (yellow box). The Medics featured within the question cards of the music box. 'Which band got to Number One with a version of the Norman Greenbaum song *Spirit In The Sky*?' We were flattered, pleased to be top of the toy-shop charts.

There was a story about Norman Greenbaum; rumour was that when he was short of money, he sold his publishing rights to the song for a paltry two hundred dollars. He retired from music completely and found himself a humble position working in a vegetarian burger restaurant in San Francisco. When Doctor and the Medics got to Number One with the same song, his song, the London based Capital Radio station called him up for an interview.

'Your song is Number One,' they enthused. 'You are going to become very wealthy.'
Norman answered politely but with a world weary tone.

'No,' he said, 'I'm not.'

He never made a cent from our version of *Spirit In The Sky*; every penny in publishing royalties (which would have been huge) was collected by the publisher who owned the song outright. What added insult to injury even further was that he was inundated with phone calls, journalists hustling for the opinion of an authentic sixties survivor. So many in fact that he couldn't do his work properly and was subsequently fired by the vegetarian restaurant.

Maybe Norman suffered the consequence of his distant association with us, The Curse of The Medics in force. Perhaps he was unwise, unsavvy in his business affairs or simply unlucky. Or maybe the song brought with it its own misfortune; like selling your soul to the devil, *Spirit In The Sky* was a song that can carry you up on a helter-skelter ride to the very top and then drop you back down with a mighty crash. That fall from grace was about to happen to me and Mr Vom.

One morning in 1988 I awoke to find a letter from the Inland Revenue, they demanded an extra thirteen thousand pounds in unpaid tax (around twenty five thousand pounds in today's money). Mr Vom received a similar demand. The Medics employed a team of accountants and bookkeepers, who kept band tax affairs in order and made sure that, as individuals, we were up to date with tax matters. No-one else in the band received these tax demands, just me and Vom; maybe, we hoped, it was a mistake.

The accountant explained that it was not a mistake. The tax inspectors had files of the band's activities since the earliest date on record, copies of old adverts, flyers and music paper clippings. They made estimations based on how much money they assumed that we should have made, and compared these estimates to the tax that we'd already paid. They wanted more. This investigation lasted for three torturous years. I had to pay the accountancy firm large sums as my accountant and the tax inspector checked every statement and receipt.

'My staff cannot be expected to work for nothing,' my accountant insisted.

The accountancy fees were never-ending. The band refused to help me as it was a personal tax demand. When I ran out of money my parents helped me out as best they could, they came out of retirement to do so, having already sold post office and bank shares (in which they invested during their working life) towards the accounts costs. Their retirement savings were also exhausted. I became a bicycle messenger to help pay these relentless invoices; one a month at first, then every week or so. Between the tax inspector and the accountant, we were cleaned out. The worry and stress was colossal. I could not talk about the ordeal without choking up, I would reduce to tears such was the strain put on me and my family.

As I discussed bankruptcy with my cash-thirsty accountant, and the Inland Revenue were informed that there was no more money to be had, miraculously the tax inspector ended his investigation. The Kafkaesque nightmare finally came to an end as suddenly as it started.

Mr Vom suffered similar torment, but neither of us understood why only he and I underwent this investigation, or why it had started in the first place. A Gossips regular who worked for the Inland Revenue confided that the tax inspector, who opened the case against us, was a fan of the band, hence his thorough collection of flyers and cuttings. In retrospect it is likely that the tax inspector was this Gossips regular himself.

Some ten years later, Vom and I were trying to source our unpaid royalty payments (neither he nor I had received any mechanical or publishing royalties since we left the band). I made some enquiries. It transpired that Mr Vom's, as well as my own missing royalties, had already been paid, to an address in Wales, Clive's address in Wales. Clive had collected our royalties. Clive was to tell a friend that he had 'kept' this money to pay some outstanding tax bills; Norman might well recognise the irony in that.

72. Leaving

Rumours abounded that Mr Vom had auditioned for indie-sex kitten Wendy James' band Transvision Vamp, as well as helping out The Babysitters and other groups on the London glam scene, plus he'd started to write music with Kris Dollimore, former guitarist from The Godfathers, under the moniker The Brotherland. I, too, had been moonlighting. Boys Wonder had a personnel change and re-recruited me into their uber-trendy ranks (I'd played a handful of gigs with them in an earlier line-up). Somewhat ruthlessly, the blatantly unfashionable McGuire was also invited to join for a short period on keyboards; he had a small 8-track studio in his flat, in which they recorded demos for nothing. This version of Boys Wonder would later morph into the band Corduroy (in which I played for 8 years), but at the time it was just a relief to be in a group without Clive's sarcasm.

Playing in two bands at once was quite possible as Medics shows were becoming far less frequent (usually just one or two a month). Boys Wonder (featuring me and McGuire) supported The Medics (featuring me and McGuire), which was fun, but The Medics were without a record deal and without credibility and were most definitely on the route to obscurity. I always maintained that I would leave the group when Vom left (my only real friend in the band), and he set his mind to leave after an altercation in a lift between Clive and some old men.

The London King's College Ball at which Mr Vom rugby-tackled Colette mid-song whilst naked and drunk (see chapter 3) was without doubt one of our most atrocious performances; we were all pissed on stage without exception (the girls finished a bottle of port each before they sound-checked). Clive splashed about the beery stage in a futile attempt to hold the attention of the inebriated students that wandered past, oblivious and resplendent in black tie, kilts and hire shop evening gowns. We didn't finish the set, let alone bother with encores.

On our departure from the college, into the quiet streets of the Aldwych, we were escorted from the building via an old and creaking lift by similarly aged security men, a handful of grey-haired gentlemen serving out their final months before retirement at an event that needed no security. They bunched around the open lift with friendly smiles and banter, pleased to be useful in some kind of work. One of these chaps, a small, kindly man with carefully combed white hair that matched the shirt of his uniform, stepped in with us, pulled the wrought-iron elevator gates closed and pressed the button to transport us the three flights to the basement. Then he made a comment about our appearance, an innocent quip at which we nodded and returned a world-weary grin - but not Clive. As the lift lurched downwards, Clive took offence, leant over the man and screamed in his face. We couldn't believe it; neither could the other security men who saw Clive bullying their colleague through the open iron gates. Wendi joined in with the needless aggression, jabbing the point of her sharp 'dragons claw' silver ring into the wrinkled veins of the poor man's neck. Clive shouted abuse at the red-faced security men puffing down the stairs to help a friend in distress, calling for backup on walkie-talkies. As the lift came to rest on the basement floor, we were greeted by the sight of twenty, sixty-something, security men, spitting on their flattened knuckles and shadow boxing against the walls, fully prepared for an old-school street fight with the disrespectful long-haired youth that they'd fought a war to protect.

We managed to escape to the van without punches being thrown. Clive laughed hard as he explained himself...

'I couldn't resist it,' he said, 'that was such fun.'

As Clive and Wendi drove away in their yellow Fiat, the rest sat in the van in stunned silence. I could see in Vom's eyes that this was the final straw.

When Mr Vom finally announced that he'd had enough, I gave my notice also but reluctantly agreed to play two final shows, both without Mr Vom.
A session drummer named Monty filled in during these final gigs, a nice enough chap but chalk and cheese compared to Mr V.

Our departure from The Medics did not however signal a new era for the health of my liver. Mr Vom would frequently visit me at my flat in Blackheath, unannounced, unabashed and up to mischief.

73. Toy box

There would be no respite; if Mr Vom appeared at my doorstep on one of his impromptu post-Medics visits, life would remain messy. I had a 'toy box'. A trunk filled with silly things to play with and dress-up in (wigs, hats, masks, fun stuff when entertaining). Mr Vom was fond of squeezing his head into these things; he found an elasticated skateboard elbow-pad particular inviting. He'd often struggle with the rubberised tube, forcing his head through the tiny opening until his mouth popped through a small gap in the padded material, lips tightly rolled back, pink and sore. His teeth protruded and gums bulged, with saliva foaming around the edges as he groaned from the force of the vice-like pressure to his head; he looked like a cross between the Alien bursting from John Hurt's stomach and a demented hedgehog.

Vom also liked smashing things or things being smashed. He once suggested that Clive (who'd arrived uninvited and with an entourage after a local gig) should smash a ukulele over his head, which Clive did with relish, shattering the instrument over Vom's nut in one blow. Flushed with success and still conscious, Vom looked for more breakables. Clive then smashed a glass vase over Vom's head; he was just about to crack an empty wine bottle over Vom's tender skull when Monique (Vom's girlfriend in tow) stepped in and stopped the violence. Clive left soon after, and Mr Vom produced a full bottle of Bourbon.

The following morning I awoke with a monster hangover on a total stranger's sticky floor in a grotty flat in a high-rise estate at the far end of The Old Kent Road, clutching a drained Bourbon bottle. I had no idea how I'd got there, or who the stranger was, but I scrounged some coins for bus fare and returned to Blackheath to find my flat all but destroyed.

The room was strewn with shards of glass and splinters of box-wood. Dirty footprints marked the white walls running up and above head height. Several large dents peppered the plaster and wallpaper flapped from the corners of the room. The carpet was patterned with dried puddles of melted candle wax. The entire contents of the toy box was ripped, torn or burnt, and Mr Vom and Monique were happily asleep in my bed. I collapsed on the sofa to sleep off my hangover, until I was woken by Vom shaking my shoulder.

'Thanks for last night, Dickie. See you soon.'

Some weeks later, after I'd finally repaired and redecorated my flat, there was a knock on the door, it was a short figure wearing a full-face helmet; Mr Vom had purchased a motorbike.

74. Beers of the world

We wheeled our heavy shopping trolley back and forth along the supermarket isle and selected two bottles of each continental lager that it had to offer. This latest of Mr Vom's visits was not to be squandered; we were to utilise our time in careful scientific study.

'Which out of all of these lagers is the best?' Vom enquired.
This knowledge, once and for all, would be of interest and importance, not just to us, but quite possibly to the rest of lager enjoying humanity.

'Beers of the world,' he noted, proudly.

We marked out a chart on a sheet of A2 paper, ruled into labelled boxes, beer names at the top and categories down the edge (taste, strength, label aesthetics etc). At the very top of the page we wrote 'Beers Of The World' and underlined it carefully; only then did we begin our mission.

We sipped and savoured, marking each delicious beverage out of ten for each category. Then we arranged the empty bottles, lined in order of rating, highest to the left. We opened each fresh bottle with respect and decorum, giggling a little harder at the futility of our work.

'Beers of the world!'

'Full bodied and crisp', we made notes in the box for that purpose, 'clear and refreshing.'

'BEERS OF THE WORLD!' we roared as the bottles were drained.

Having sampled and rated many, many beers of the world, lined up the empties in order of preference and completed the chart, we finally had our winner. Our top three were, in reverse order:

Peroni Nastro Azzurro.

Birra Moretti.

Czech Budweiser Budvar.

A special note of excellence was also awarded to Pilsner Urquell and Carlsberg Elephant beer. We were excited with our results and resolved to frame and hang The Beers Of The World chart on my wall.

My girlfriend, Madeleine, phoned to say she was coming round, and that I should probably eat something if Mr Vom was staying, she understood us both well. The cupboards were empty so I decided to pop to a late night grocer to buy a frozen pizza to soak up the alcohol.

'Get a bottle of Jack Daniel's, Dickie,' Mr Vom shouted, as I wobbled down the road on my mountain bike.

On my return I put the frozen pepperoni pizza in the oven and handed Vom his bottle of bourbon.

'Glasses?'

I handed Mr Vom two clean pint glasses into which he emptied the full bottle of Jack Daniel's, divided equally, just over half pint in each.

'Cheers.'

We downed the half pints of whiskey in one go, then we ate the pizza, and I retired to bed. Mr Vom took the sofa.

I slept fitfully; my slumber was disturbed by bad dreams and muscle spasms. I was vaguely aware of screaming during the early hours, which also woke me briefly, but I returned to sleep until the morning, when the phone rang next to my bed; it was Mads.

'I've already phoned your work and told them that you are not going in today, because you're sick,' she said.
I was starting, that morning, with a new cycle courier firm (I'd become a cycle courier during the tax inspection ordeal). It was really bad form to miss the first day of a new job, but Mads was strangely correct, I didn't feel very well.

Mr Vom was up and about.

'There's only one Dickie Damage,' he was singing at the top of his voice, 'there's only one Dickie Damage... there's only one Dickie Dammmaaaage.'
I sat up in bed, my head felt like it had been kicked by a rugby team.

'Mads came in last night - ha, ha, but she left,' Vom laughed as he stood in the bedroom doorway, fiddling with his hair. 'She screamed, really loudly, ha, ha, like in a horror film.'
I was confused, why was Mads screaming, why had she left?

'Why, what have you done?' I asked.

'Me? Nothing.' He zipped up his leather jacket. 'Anyway, I'm off now, Dickie Damage.' Vom picked up his motorbike helmet and opened the front door to leave. 'BEERS OF THE WORLD!' he said.

It was some hours before I felt well enough to get out of bed, snatching onto furniture and steadying myself against the walls as I slowly made my way to the bathroom. I was in for a terrible shock. The smell was atrocious, overwhelming and pungent. Very little daylight was penetrating the bathroom window, the glass so completely obscured; the floor was glistening with what natural light had managed to shine between the gaps, as were the walls and parts of the ceiling. A dense wet substance coated the surfaces. I pulled a light cord, switched on the electric light and gasped with utter shock. Every inch of the small tiled bathroom was covered, almost in its entirety, with thick rusty-brown vomit. It looked like the walls, floor and ceiling had been spray-painted with whiskey-coloured puke. Small flecks of pepperoni dotted the fetid viscous matter, defying gravity as it stubbornly coated the vertical surfaces. Only the occasional sound of moist drips broke the otherwise silent apparition, as the heavier lumps sagged and dropped from the ceiling, plopping into the lake of stinking sick on the floor.

Madeleine had arrived in the night, experienced this dreadful sight and ran, but not before screaming with utter revulsion. Apparently, Mr Vom didn't even get a chance to say hello.

75. Conclusions

An hour or so before Mr Vom deflowered Colette's
cousin, behind a pine tree in the Italian Alps in '86, he
participated in a friendly game of five-pin bowling
with the locals. He didn't bowl the wooden bowing
ball towards the skittles however; he ran down the
alley and kicked them flying, booting them across the
field in a spray of hand-whittled wood and varnish.
The players were shocked and shouted foreign
profanities, but Mr Vom defused the situation by
eating bumble bees, plucked from nearby wild
flowers; the dying insect buzzed at Vom's lips as he
grinned inanely. The mystified locals assumed that he
was 'simple in the head' and handed the bowling ball
back to the impish little fellow, to humour him.

*

During a concert in Finsbury Park in August 1987,
headlined by Hawkwind called 'Acid Daze', I witness
one of the singers from grunge pin-ups Pop Will Eat
Itself unconscious on the floor of the back-stage
hospitality tent, whilst his fellow band members
circled around and urinated on him. I didn't find this
particularly shocking, a few days prior I'd watched Mr
Vom drink from a pint of Clive's warm piss.

*

Harry D'mac made the acquaintance of a Rolling
Stone Magazine journalist near the end of our US tour;
she took us to a private party in an exclusive nightclub

on the top floor of a New York skyscraper, where Jeff Beck and Eric Clapton were playing on-stage with various NY session musicians. McGuire and I were invited to get up and 'jam a few numbers'; we politely agreed, but whilst instruments were prepared for us on-stage, we literally ran from the premises. Mr Vom didn't join us because he was bed-ridden; where he was to stay for several feverish days, delirious in sweat soaked bedding with concerned doctors busied at his side. He'd contracted Legionnaires' Disease from hotel air conditioning.

*

Mr Vom noticed some paparazzi loitering outside Stringfellows after pub hours one evening; he assumed that there must be adventures to be had inside but was refused entry. The photographers bunched around a limousine pulling up in front of the club. A passenger climbed from the car and entered Stringfellows – but not before Mr Vom grabbed the unsuspecting fellow's crotch and grinned for the cameras. The following morning there was a headline in a tabloid newspaper, 'Ruffian assaults Lord Linley'. There was an accompanying photograph – Mr Vom grabbing Viscount Linley's bollocks.

*

Reminiscences are all that remain of my time in Doctor and the Medics with Mr Vom. We did not make as much money as people naturally assume or that we were led to believe. Vom's parents asked Andrew King how much money their son could expect to make from spending four weeks at Number One in the UK charts.

'Oh, easily enough for a house,' Andrew answered confidently.

We didn't make enough for a house, far from it, and once the Inland Revenue had finished with us, Vom and I were flat broke.

Around the time of our parting company with IRS, management exercised an option in the contract to audit (officially inspect) the record label accounts, Andrew King reckoned that they had under-accounted; *Spirit In The Sky* was a hit in eighteen counties and sold almost two and a half million units worldwide; we should have received more money. The findings found in favour of IRS, they had a contractual clause which permitted cross-collateralisation (profits made in the UK could be offset against losses suffered internationally). Our highest chart position in America was sixty-nine; despite being awarded silver discs for chart sales in the UK, gold for other European territories and platinum in Australia, IRS made a loss with The Medics in the US, which swallowed up the cash.

Memories cloud and fade with time, friendship can experience a similar fate; fortunately my friendship with Mr Vom has, despite the toxins imbibed that served to lessen those memories, survived the years. The adventure of sharing success in a rock group is one that, in our case at least, was about experiencing the moment; everything else is fleeting. Money, fame and success, they are illusions. Mr Vom is my brother, and that is real and truly to be treasured; long may our adventures continue.

End.

The Absurdist

by Richard Searle

The Absurdist is a light hearted, science-fictional tale about the illusionary nature of reality, lethal cocktails, hairy heroes, unrequited love and wasp hammers. Rude and irreverent, this funny philosophical caper, about two young scam-artists caught up in unusual events, features the prettiest of girls, silliest of toys, quantum physics and giant space propellers in an adventure of absurd proportions.

Sketchistentialism

by Richard Searle

'Sketch – noun,
a drawing or cartoon, usually humorous, as in a
newspaper or periodical, symbolising, satirising, or
caricaturing some action, subject, or person of popular
interest.'

'Existentialism – noun,
of life, death and religion, a modern philosophical
movement stressing the importance of personal
experience, responsibility and the demands that they
make on the individual, who is seen as a free agent in a
deterministic and seemingly meaningless universe.'

'Sketchistentialism – book,
a collection of cartoon art from the pen of Richard
Searle.'

Printed in Great Britain
by Amazon.co.uk, Ltd.,
Marston Gate.